Everywhere

STEVE
ADDISON

Also by Steve Addison

Movements That Change the World:
Five Keys to Spreading the Gospel (2009)

What Jesus Started: Joining the Movement,
Changing the World (2012)

Pioneering Movements: Leadership That Multiplies
Disciples and Churches (2015)

The Rise and Fall of Movements: A Roadmap for Leaders (2019)

Your Part in God's Story: 40 Days from Genesis to Revelation (2021)

Acts and the Movement of God: From Jerusalem to the
Ends of the Earth (2023)

In *Everywhere*, Steve Addison offers a bold and deeply challenging vision of the global movement of God, reminding us that mission always requires risk and faith. Through powerful true stories—from families persevering in war-torn Iraq to men discovering hope on death row in Texas—Addison shows that ordinary people, convinced that Jesus is worth it all, are the catalytic force behind gospel multiplication.

Grounded in Scripture and brought vividly to life in today's world, *Everywhere* reveals how movements are ignited by the Word and the Spirit. This book provides a clear and compelling roadmap for church leaders ready to move beyond maintenance and into missional movement. If you're willing to trade the comfort of the status quo for God's ultimate, glorious vision, this book is essential reading.

Dave Ferguson, CEO of Exponential;

author of *Hero Maker*, *B.L.E.S.S.*, and *Multiplier*

Powerful and practical! Journey with Steve Addison to see how God is using kingdom movements to transform lives in the most unlikely places: from Texas death row to Communist Laos and Muslim Iran—*Everywhere!* This is one of the best books I've read for its vivid stories, combining seamlessly with practical actions that every disciple can implement.

David Garrison, missionary;

author of *Church Planting Movements*

and *A Wind in the House of Islam*

Filled with important principles and powerful illustrations from movements emerging around the world, *Everywhere* will inspire and equip you. Whether you are new to disciple-multiplication or you've been at it for years, the challenge and lessons this book offers will be of great value.

Cynthia Anderson, host of *Dare to Multiply Podcast*;

author of *The Multiplier's Mindset*

In *Everywhere*, Steve Addison does a masterful job of weaving small personal stories into an overarching tapestry of what God is doing all around the world to multiply disciples and churches.

But this book is more than just inspiring stories. Since these are stories about real people, Steve also describes the various sins, struggles, challenges, and failures that individuals and teams have experienced along the way.

His analysis of key principles shows us how we can learn from the patterns of God's work in these contexts and adapt them to our own situations. I wholeheartedly recommend you read this book and share it with others.

Stan Parks, coauthor of *Forests in the Seed*

Repeatedly, as I read *Everywhere*, I thought, *This could be the New Testament church*. And that's the point. And that's why this book is so inspirational. Steve Addison draws principles from these stories of movements and develops them using the patterns found in Scripture. He helps us see how Jesus continues to build his church as a missionary disciple making movement today, and how we can join in his mission.

Each context is expertly researched and recorded, and the faith, sacrifice, and courage of these missional leaders will move you to tears and set your heart on fire. This book confirms Steve Addison as an international expert on movements, and provides a vital window into what God is doing around the world.

John McGinley, director of Myriad church planting initiative; author of *Awaken*

First, I must confess that I would endorse anything Steve wrote without asking any questions. Second, whatever I've written in principle, Steve has sussed out in practice, scouring the world and church history to give us real-world examples. This latest book shifts from movements as a whole to explore the core practice of movement-making—making disciples—and it's worth the read.

Peyton Jones, author of *Discipology* and *Church Plantology*

Everywhere

How God

Multiplies

Disciples &

Churches

STEVE ADDISON

100 MOVEMENTS
PUBLISHING

To Noy and Chantha

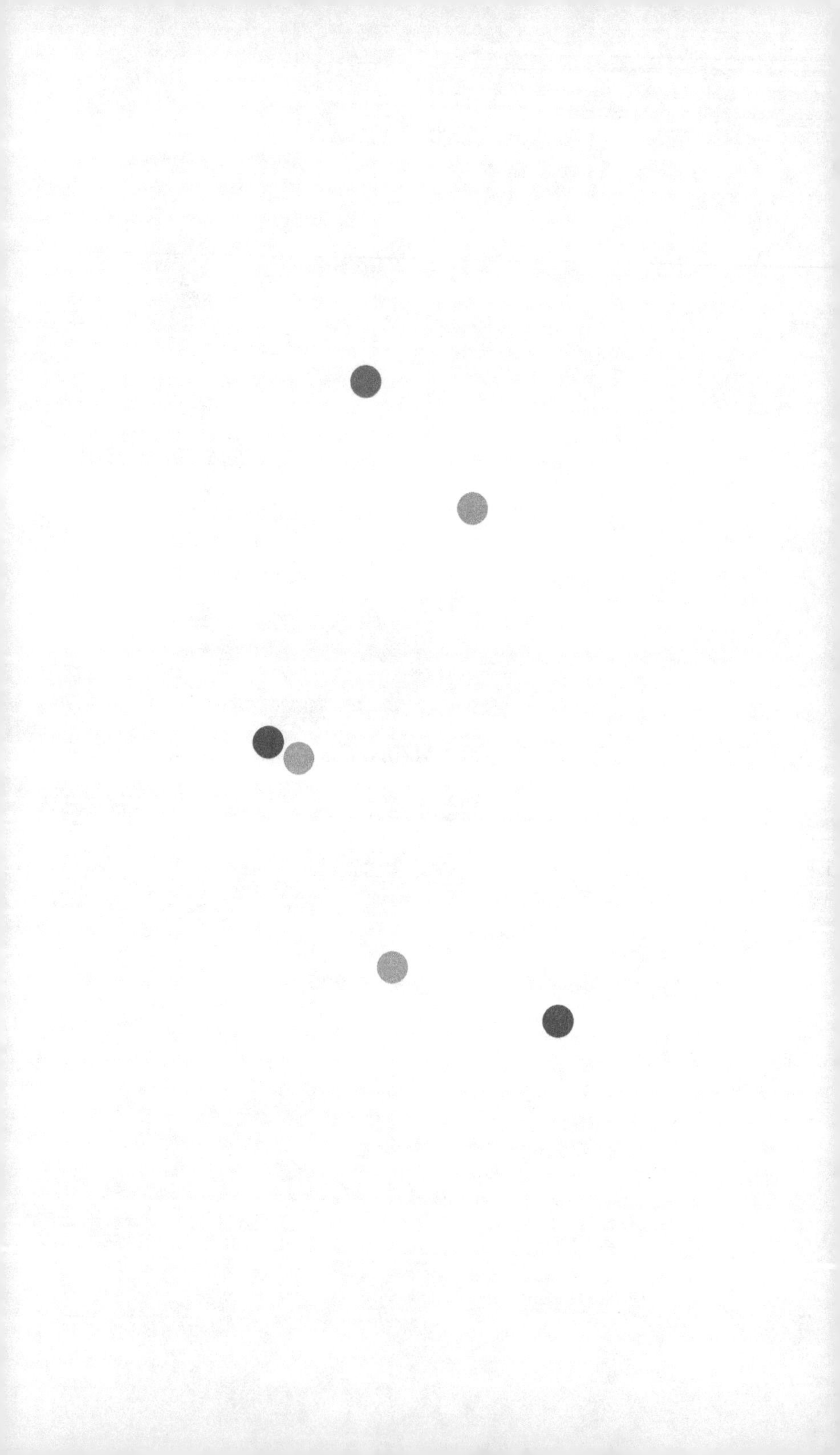

Contents

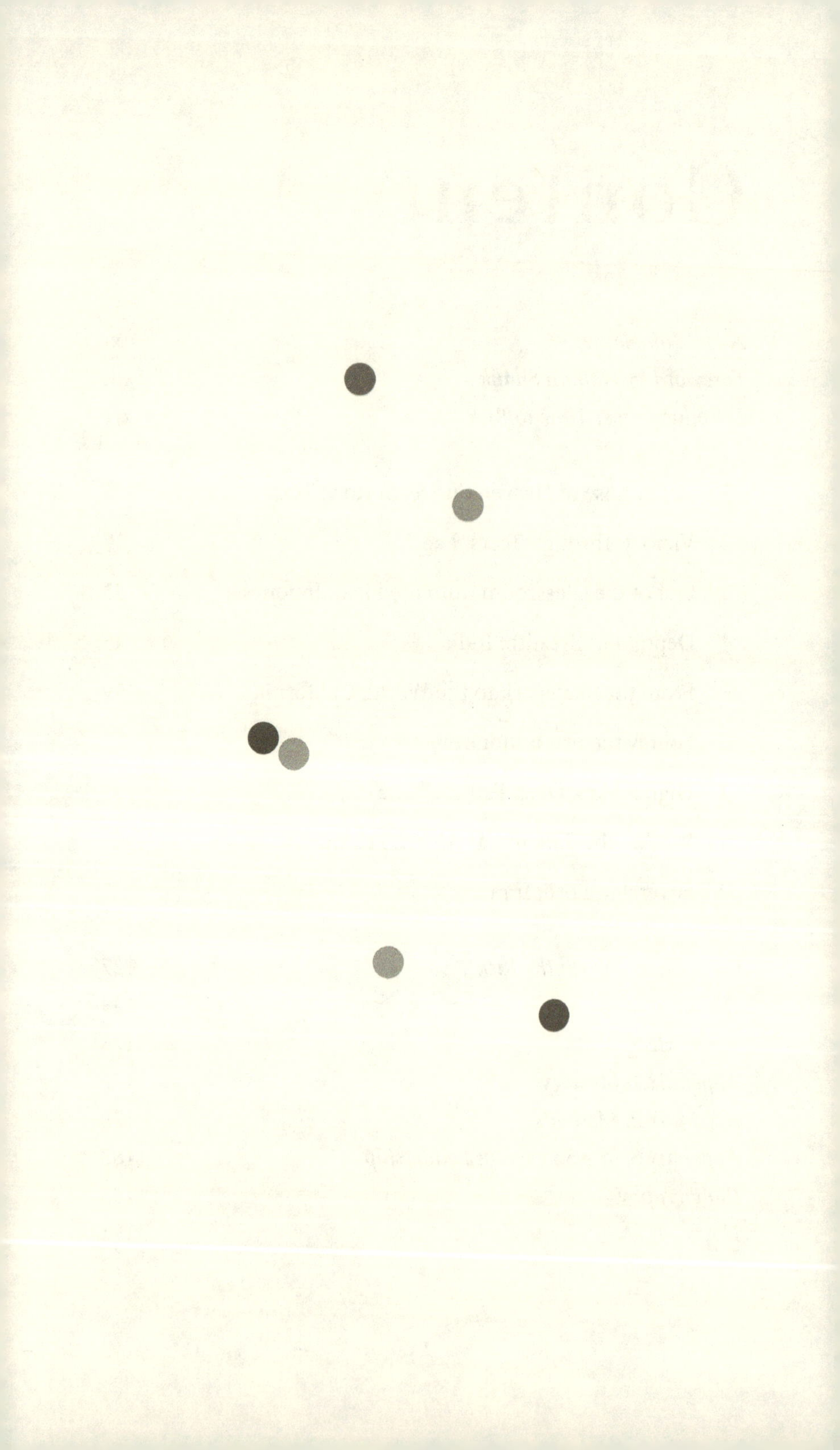

A Note on Names

Many of the individuals featured in this book are working in sensitive and hostile environments. To protect them, I have used first-name pseudonyms. When I use a first name and surname, the name is real.

Foreword

I have known Steve Addison for nearly two decades. From our first conversation, I have found him to be a voracious learner—firing questions and eager for any testimony that points to the ways of our Ruler, Jesus. I have been personally served by Steve's encouragement, at times admonished by his wisdom and fidelity to Scripture, and certainly inspired by his faithful walk. I am not alone. Steve has many friends like me. It is out of these relationships that this book has grown; what lies before you is but a sample of the testimonies God has used Steve to gather.

As you read Steve's collection, you will recognize certain patterns. For example, God uses simple people (1 Corinthians 1:26–31). Acknowledging this fact has enabled Steve to consistently boast in the Lord (v.31) with eyes that see those overlooked by the world. Furthermore, Steve understands that kingdom advance is typically paralleled by hardship and persecution. This should come as no surprise, as it is promised throughout the New Testament (John 16:33; 2 Timothy 3:12), yet the stories included here are a timely reminder. What might be new to you in these examples is the pattern of multiplication. For Steve, the pattern is not only observable; it is expected as the fruit of dependence on the Spirit's power and fidelity to biblical principles.

As you consider these stories, you might ask: What other pathway to genuine multiplication might we expect?

I am often surprised how multiplication is viewed—at times even disregarded—as merely an option, a fad, a method, or the fruit of excessive pragmatism. Meanwhile, the biblical record teaches, demonstrates, and even commands what we still see unfolding among the nations today: the multiplication of disciples and churches.

As you read this book, you might consider the question: Does Jesus' mobilization of his disciples in the New Testament demonstrate multiplication?

The identification and sending of the Twelve in Luke 9 was immediately followed by Jesus' mobilization of "seventy-two others" in Luke 10. Notably, the first instruction for these thirty-six pairs was that they simply were not enough! Jesus said to them, "The harvest is plentiful, but the workers are few. Ask the Lord of the harvest, therefore, to send out workers into his harvest field" (Luke 10:2). A ripe harvest demanded such a petition, and Jesus clearly expected the Lord of the harvest to answer it. The lesson for these laborers was dependence on the Lord. Such prayer required vision beyond their efforts and human means, acknowledging that the harvest force must scale to meet the harvest opportunity.

Similarly, the Great Commission anticipates and even expects multiplication as disciples become disciple makers. The cyclical secret of Matthew 28:18–20 is that Christ's authority and presence are with every disciple for the sake of making more disciples. As we go, baptize, and teach disciples to obey all that Jesus commanded, they also take up the command—they too receive the commission to make disciples of the nations.

This cycle of multiplication continued throughout the book of Acts, where Luke's pen details a Spirit-compelled mission and ministry. The result? The itinerancy of those sent and scattered led to the engagement of unreached peoples and places, the sowing of gospel seed, the making of disciples, the forming of churches, and the multiplication of leaders who could repeat the process … everywhere.

The One with all authority in heaven and on earth remains with us even to the end of the age (Matthew 28:20). His commission stands as the nations await the announcement of his reign. The call to make and multiply disciples remains a stewardship for every generation until the Lord's appearing. The book before you assumes Jesus continues to multiply disciples through disciple makers.

As you read this book, you might consider the question: Does God still work this way today?

The existence of significant Christian populations currently found around the world is evidence of historic multiplication. Consider the fact that the world's population did not reach 1 billion until the year 1804. At that time, evangelical faith was largely limited to a small number of populations, primarily in the Western hemisphere. By 2022, the world's population passed 8 billion, with 9 billion expected by 2037. It therefore follows that over the past two hundred years, wherever genuine Christ-followers have grown from 1 to 2 percent of a local population, they must have multiplied.[1] This is true of any significant population of Christians around the world. Wherever genuine Christian communities have grown as a percentage of the population, there is but one pathway: disciples multiplying disciples.

One reason this is so hard to grasp in the West is that many of us have not seen such multiplication in our lifetime. The United States, for example, has not seen church growth keep up with population growth since the 1950s. This means most Americans have only known a church in decline. At times, this reality may fuel suspicion or even criticism of harvest fields seeing rapid growth. It's easy to be skeptical of what we have never seen. Yet the undeniable growth of the global church owes its existence to a growth rate that, at some point, outstripped general population growth.

This is why books like this matter. Across Scripture, we are admonished, encouraged, and in fact called to trust God for what we cannot, or do not yet, see. Any collection of the promises of God across Scripture immediately illustrates that faith is the catalyst for bold action. As believers, we can hold fast to the truth that God is committed to this mission; in fact, the character of our God is at stake. Either he keeps his promise of a vast *multitude* from every nation, tribe, people, and language, or his Word is proven false, his character is impugned, and his glory diminished (Revelation 7:9–10). Because we know he is faithful, we can read the accounts in these pages with confidence; they allow us to "see" the very promises we have been called to trust.

Finally, as you read this book, you might ask: Why this book? What makes Steve Addison's effort worthy of our attention?

Consistent with both the Galilean ministry of Christ and the post-Pentecost examples of Christ's first followers, Steve calls readers to consider both personal and corporate stewardship from entry to exit. With this book (and indeed with much of Steve's writing), he champions a fully orbed missionary and church-planting task. While books abound on various components of mission or church planting, Steve calls for and, in fact, evaluates each case study through his summary of biblical "method." According to Steve, pioneering among the lost demands entry into new fields and gospel seed-sowing. Such pioneering must be followed by discipleship, church formation, and leadership development.

I believe that this matters because the New Testament demonstrates multiplication from church to church. From the Jerusalem church, those scattered established the church in Antioch (Acts 11:19–21). From Antioch, sent ones established the Galatian churches (Acts 13:1–14, 23). From a Galatian church at Lystra, a disciple named Timothy joined the apostolic effort, and churches in Macedonia and Achaia were the fruit (Acts 16–18). I trust you will benefit from Steve's assessment and commitment to this pattern.

Finally, Steve's writing (here and elsewhere) demonstrates the balance between a disciple's responsibility and utter dependence on God to produce fruit. In South Asia, where I have spent much of my life, we seek to mobilize gospel labor within the "controllables" of the kingdom. To be sure, kingdom advance depends upon much that is beyond our control. As Paul reminded the Corinthians, he and Apollos may have sown and watered, but it is only God who gives the increase (1 Corinthians 3:6–7). So it is with any kingdom stewardship. Disciples put their hands to a very real plow of responsibility in sowing and reaping. Yet, no farmer in any generation has the ability to give life to the seed. Steve not only grasps this reality, but he also encourages those who desire multiplication with a consistent balance of personal obedience and dependence on the Lord of the harvest.

As you read, consider the boldness required to engage a pioneer field. Consider the faith and priority required to scatter the gospel consistently amidst the lost. Is not the commitment of time and effort to follow up believers with biblical discipleship a "controllable"? Are we not responsible for applying the Lord's expectation for function, authority, leadership, and instruction as we form churches? Is not the equipping and surrender of new leaders the fruit of intentional investment?

Steve calls his readers to such "controllable" preparation and obedience. Balanced against such disciplined investment is faith. Only God prepares and convicts the heart. Only God gives life to the seed. Only God empowers disciples, births churches, and gifts leaders for service. The disciple maker is dependent on God for these "uncontrollables" of kingdom advance. The good news is that God has commissioned and is present in the enterprise. In reading and applying this book, you will be inspired and equipped to join *him* in multiplying disciples and churches … everywhere.

Nathan Shank
Senior advisor of Strategy and Implementation, International Mission Board; coauthor of *The Four Fields of Kingdom Growth*

Introduction

A Time to Risk

Then the church throughout Judea, Galilee and Samaria enjoyed a time of peace and was strengthened. Living in the fear of the Lord and encouraged by the Holy Spirit, it increased in numbers.

ACTS 9:31

In 2016, just as Joe and Dawn decided to move to northern Iraq, news broke over their car radio: ISIS had brutally murdered Christians in the region that would soon be their home.

How would this horrific news impact their decision? What would they do? Dawn was no stranger to the risks of serving in Iraq. Ten years earlier, she had worked in the country, but she was single then. Now, she and Joe were married with two young children. However, they resolved not to walk away from the call to make Jesus known, convinced that he is worth it all.

This resolution is at the heart of any movement: ordinary people moving toward people far from God, because Jesus is worth it all.

The story of Joe and Dawn is not an isolated one; it is a pattern. Over the past few years, I've been on a search for signs of the movement of God. This search has taken me to distant places—from war-torn Lebanon to the suburbs of California, and from the prisons of Texas to the villages of Communist Laos. Whether in Islamic Iran, Hindu India, or Muslim Indonesia, I've been gathering stories and case studies.

During a ten-day road trip through India, I met countless people eager to share their stories of forgiveness, healing, and lasting peace within families. A dad who had once been a drunkard had become a devoted husband and father—a transformation I heard repeated in many households. Elsewhere, a widow abandoned by the roadside is now following Christ and making disciples.

In Texas, I heard God's praises sung by murderers on death row. Men who were once deadly rivals had become brothers in Christ, and now they are multiplying disciples within the prison walls and beyond.

In Laos, I met a widow whose husband was murdered by government agents. For twenty years, she has continued his work of winning disciples and planting churches in a country under hostile Communist rule.

This book is filled with similar testimonies—story after story of God at work, reshaping one heart, one family, one network, and one generation at a time. It's these stories of transformation that point to a genuine movement of God.

In the Beginning

When Jesus rose from the dead, he encountered disciples who had failed him—people just like us. He didn't just forgive them; he transformed them into a missionary movement. Jesus gave them his Word, promised them his Spirit, and clarified their mission. This gospel of repentance and forgiveness of sins exploded out from Jerusalem, spreading to every corner of the known world and beginning the mission to reach every place and every people group. Empowered by the Spirit, Jesus' first disciples boldly proclaimed the gospel, baptizing those who believed and teaching them to obey everything Jesus commanded. Ordinary people and their stories fill the pages of the Gospels and Acts. In these accounts, the movement of God is clear. Its presence can be identified by its fruit.

Since the day of Pentecost, the Word has been spreading through ordinary people empowered by the Spirit. Wherever the Word and Spirit go, the result is disciples and churches that bring glory to God.

And it's still happening today.

During their eight years in northern Iraq, Joe and Dawn spread the gospel, identified leaders among the new disciples, and trained them to reproduce disciples and churches. But life in the country was far from certain. Missiles fell near their home. Disciples were persecuted. Some were killed. They learned that, while events may seem out of control, God is still on his throne.

This is what Jesus predicted (Matthew 24:3–14). He warned that wars, famine, and natural disasters would plague the time between his first and second comings. It would be a time when his disciples were hated and persecuted—a world of false prophets, deception, and evil, where the love of most would grow cold. But this season of hardship is not the final word. Jesus announced that the gospel would be preached to all nations, and then the end would come.

This final, glorious vision is the compass that set Joe and Dawn's course. It is the reason they exchanged the security of home for the uncertainty of war-torn northern Iraq and relocated their family across the globe.

Their sacrifice was anchored in a certain future, for we know where history is going. There is a multitude standing before the throne of God, from every nation, tribe, language, and people, worshipping the Lamb that was slain. This is what the end looks like. This is why Jesus suffered and rose—to launch a movement of God that will reveal his glory to every people group and in every place, and from them, to gather a people to himself.

Movements Today

The world Jesus predicted is the world we inhabit. It is hard to ignore the weight of the headlines, the cultural resistance, and the cynicism—all of which can make our love grow cold. But this is not a time for withdrawal; it is a time of opportunity because God is at work. The patterns are there in Scripture, and they are on display in the disciple making movements across the globe. Are we willing to apply the lessons?

The disciple making movements in these pages have multiple streams of at least fourth-generation churches composed of new believers: One church plants another, which plants another, and so on. Four generations across multiple streams.

Research shows that "many movements fade away before reaching multiple generations, but those that reach multiple generations become a powerful, nearly unstoppable force."[1] Over the last thirty years, the number of disciples in these movements has increased from 10,000 in 1995 to over 100 million in 2024.[2] These numbers alone should get our attention.

For over thirty years, I've been studying movements, looking for patterns, distilling principles, and sharing lessons and accounts. This book tells the stories of nine unstoppable movements across the globe. I spent a year with practitioners in their environments, traveling, listening, watching, and learning. I conducted online interviews and, when research and records were available, I read them.

This book is the product of that journey.

I have two hopes in writing. First, I want you to hear from the practitioners and learn from their example. They are the experts.

They lead the way in doing what Christ commanded, often at high cost. Second, I want you to see the glory of God in their struggles and victories. Jesus is risen, and he still leads the way as his Word spreads in the power of the Holy Spirit through his people.

Movement Dynamics

Movements rise and fall based on their alignment with the life and ministry of Jesus. He is the standard. As you read the stories in the following chapters, you'll notice the recurring patterns that align with the life and ministry of Jesus in the Gospels and Acts. Movements are shaped by three elements: *Identity*, *Strategy*, and *Methods*.[3]

Identity

Jesus' baptism and wilderness testing reveal the core *Identity* of the movement he started. The Son *obeyed the Father's Word, relied on the Holy Spirit*, and remained *faithful to the core missionary task*. Following his victory, he restored the disciples by teaching them from the Word, promising the Holy Spirit, and reminding them of their mission—multiplying disciples and churches worldwide.

Obedient to the Word. Jesus came to fulfill the Scriptures. He placed his life and ministry under the authority of God's living Word, expressing his love through complete obedience. The story of the movement of God in Acts is the story of the spread of God's dynamic Word. The Word spreads, increases, multiplies, and grows in power, traveling to the ends of the earth and conquering the world. Wherever the Word goes, the fruit is new disciples and new churches.

Dependent on the Holy Spirit. The same Spirit who hovered over the waters at Creation was the agent of Jesus' conception. At his baptism, the Spirit descended on Jesus as he was praying, anointing him with power and authority to carry out his mission. Jesus, filled with the Spirit, overcame Satan in the wilderness and, in the power of the Spirit, returned to begin his ministry. At Pentecost, the Spirit fell upon every disciple, and they proclaimed the glory of God, revealed in Jesus. The Word went out in the power of the Spirit. Every believer was ordained to the ministry of bearing witness to the world. It's the Spirit who disrupts comfort and propels God's people into mission.

Faithful to the mission. The story of the Bible is the story of God's mission to win back a people for himself. Through his death, he purchased a people for God from every tribe, language, people, and nation. From his position of supreme authority, Jesus gave his followers a universal mission—to make disciples of all nations. In Acts, the Spirit and the Word propel the mission forward through ordinary people. The result is disciples and churches bringing glory to God everywhere.

Strategy

Jesus expressed his *Identity* through action. We can see a consistent pattern in the *Strategy* Jesus employed and how he trained his disciples.[4]

1. Entry: Jesus came to seek and save the lost

Movements cross boundaries to connect with people far from God. They don't wait for people to approach them. Instead, they actively seek God-prepared insiders who are open to the gospel and well-connected within their community.

2. Gospel: Jesus proclaimed and demonstrated the good news of the kingdom

Movements share the good news of Jesus through proclamation, demonstration, and teaching. They equip new disciples to become the channels through which the good news spreads to their communities.

3. Disciples: Jesus called people to follow and obey him

Movements lead people to faith in Jesus Christ (conversion, baptism, gift of the Holy Spirit) and teach them to follow Jesus' commands, including the command to make disciples.

4. Churches: Jesus gathered and built a new community centered on his life and teaching

Movements help new disciples establish churches modeled after Acts 2:36–47.[5] These churches operate under the authority of the apostles' teaching, and they learn to pray, worship, love one another, care for the poor, and make disciples. Local leaders are identified and developed.

5. Leaders: Jesus modeled and commissioned others to do the same work

Missionary movements train local leaders and send out mobile apostolic teams into new, unreached fields to advance the spread of the gospel.

Movements embrace the whole picture, not just one of these five elements—not just the local community but the world. Not just evangelism but disciples. Not just disciples but churches. Not just leaders but multiplying leaders.

Methods

Jesus' communication and ministry *Methods* were contextually relevant. His sayings and stories were easily transmitted as the missionary movement advanced from person to person. The movement he began spread from Jerusalem to Rome on a minimal budget, primarily through receptive households.

Jesus trained his disciples in the field using *Methods* that were reproducible and transferable. He did not impose unnecessary restrictions on who could be trusted to make disciples. Movements thrive when disciples adopt simple, reproducible, and affordable methods that spread the Word, develop new disciples, strengthen churches, and release new leaders.

This outline of *Identity*, *Strategy*, and *Methods* provides a framework for understanding each case study. At the end of each chapter, there is a reflection on how these dynamics are evident in the stories, along with a guide for applying the lessons learned. The *Deeper Studies* at the end of the book explore essential themes raised by the case studies and are designed for group discussion, learning, and application.

Risk Everything!

Jesus told a story about a man who went on a journey and entrusted different amounts of gold to three servants. Two of the servants invested the money and earned a profit for their master. When he returned, he praised and rewarded them. Then the man who had received one bag of gold came and said, "Master … I knew that you are a hard man, harvesting where you have not sown and gathering where you have not scattered seed. So I was afraid and went out and hid your gold in the ground. See, here is what belongs to you" (Matthew 25:24–25).

This servant missed the chance to take a risk and make a profit for his master. He didn't misuse the money; he buried it. He played it safe and lost his opportunity to participate in his master's work.

Jesus will return and hold us accountable for how we've used what he's given us. Following him isn't just about crossing the finish line; he has something for us to do. We need to know his purposes and risk everything to fulfill them. We have one brief life to live and all eternity to celebrate our victories. This book is filled with people who have taken those risks and given their all to Jesus. Will we do the same?

God is working in the world to gather a people for himself. He invites us to join what he is doing. It's God's story, but we all have a part to play. You might not be called to serve in a war zone, minister on death row, or plant churches under hostile Communist rule. Perhaps it starts closer to home: with your family, on your street, at work, or among your friends. We all have different callings and abilities. The question is, what will you do with what God has given you?

Read the stories in whatever order you prefer. Learn the lessons. Be inspired by how God uses ordinary people to fulfill his mission—disciples and churches to the glory of God. Everywhere.

A Glimpse of Heaven on Death Row

Texas

He has sent me to bind up the brokenhearted, to proclaim freedom for the captives and release from darkness for the prisoners.

ISAIAH 61:1

There are 1.8 million people behind bars in the United States, giving it the largest prison population in the world. In Texas—the state with the greatest number of inmates—the most notorious offenders are held on death row at the Polunsky Unit.

I entered death row and stood behind the yellow line that kept me from the bars. This was my first time inside any prison, and the statistics suddenly became a heavy, cold reality.[1]

Eight men in white prison garb stood waiting—white, Black, Hispanic, and Asian, a condemned mosaic of faces, each one sentenced to death for murder.

Someone called out from the rows of steel, "Can we sing?"

The familiar words echoed throughout the unit as they sang the Lord's Prayer.

I had expected despair and ruin, but on the other side of the bars were men vibrant with the life of Christ. In that bleak corridor, I experienced a taste of heaven on death row, the glory of God shining from each of the inmates. I longed to cross that yellow line, put my hands through the bars, and embrace my brothers.

"We don't call this death row," they told me. "We call it life row. This is where we found Jesus."

Each man awaits his execution date—a wait that could last months or decades. When the time comes, they face death by lethal injection. Yet each time the guards escort a condemned brother, these disciples stand in their cells, singing "Amazing Grace" as he leaves.

In the last three years, twenty of the twenty-four men executed at Polunsky were followers of Jesus who came to faith on death row. Today, eighty of the 168 men awaiting execution are believers who have planted churches in six of the fourteen sections of Polunsky.

Elsewhere, in one of the other maximum-security units, prisoner-led churches regularly gather in day rooms. The night we were there, we joined the disciples in the prison chapel. As a band played and a choir led, 150 men raised their voices in unified worship to God—another glimpse of heaven, confirming that this is not just a story of a few remarkable individuals.

This is the story of a movement of God.

Don Waybright: The Outsider

The movement began in 2012, when Darrington Prison partnered with a local seminary to launch a four-year program in Biblical Studies. This wasn't just any program; it carried a unique requirement: Only inmates serving sentences of twenty-five years or more could apply. Graduates were qualified as field ministers and could be assigned to facilities across the state.

Don Waybright, a missions pastor and seminary teacher who was an outsider to the system, seized the opportunity to teach a course focused specifically on making disciples and planting churches. Don didn't just lecture; he guided his students through the Gospels and Acts, looking at how Jesus and his disciples carried out their mission. As they read the text, they answered these questions:

- How did they enter unreached fields?
- What did they say?
- How did they make disciples?
- How did they form churches?
- How did they multiply workers?
- How will we obey what we've learned here in prison?

With the strategy clear, Don equipped the men with simple, reproducible methods for sharing the gospel. This included reading Scripture for discipleship using a 3-Thirds pattern, as well as the practical steps of how to form healthy churches and develop leaders.[2] As he coached the students, they immediately turned their learning into action.

Don discovered that the most receptive prisoners were in solitary confinement, isolated in five-by-seven-foot concrete cells for twenty-three hours a day. Yet, this didn't stop discipleship. Instead, they shouted the gospel to one another from their cells. Other inmates came to Christ just by listening to them.

By 2019, the prison had 290 churches meeting in each day room, and over seven hundred men had been baptized. As believers were transferred to other facilities, the movement spread, turning the entire state prison system into a vast new mission field.

David Ludwick: The Insider

David Ludwick, a convicted murderer serving a minimum forty-year sentence, was a student in Don's seminary program and emerged as the movement's pioneer on the inside. Ludwick was then assigned to Coffield—the state's largest prison, housing 4,800 inmates—where he partnered with Brandon Authement, a fellow field minister and skilled integrator and administrator.

David and Brandon launched a program designed for multiplying new disciples, organizing the training around the 5-Levels of Leadership in a multiplying movement.[3] The first level involves learning to obey Christ's commands: repent and believe, be baptized, love one another, celebrate the Lord's Supper, give generously, and make disciples.

The results are consistent: Every time the course runs, they typically baptize fifty to seventy new believers after just the second lesson. These disciples live out their faith in the day room. In prison, life revolves around this communal space, where inmates gather to watch TV or play cards. But in many facilities, the rooms have been transformed, becoming the epicenter of this movement. They are now the focal point where the gospel spreads, disciples are made, churches are formed, and leaders are trained. One time, an African American brother baptized a former Aryan Nation (white supremacist) inmate he had led to Christ. On another occasion, Mexican inmates risked their lives to be baptized after renouncing their gang membership.

David and Brandon's training has been accepted into the prison's Gang Renunciation and Disassociation (GRAD) program. Inmates seeking to leave their life of crime and gang membership apply to GRAD, which offers life-skills courses. David and Brandon ensure that whatever life-skills course they are assigned to teach, they eventually train participants in multiplying disciples and churches using a 4-Fields strategy.[4]

Despite opposition from some traditional chaplains and existing ministries, the prison authorities continued to support the program after witnessing its effects. "You can hear the gospel shared 24/7 in this prison," the Warden at Coffield says. "My officers are safe. This was once one of the most dangerous prisons in Texas. Nobody wanted to be transferred here. Now, inmates *want* to get transferred here."

Terry Solley: Breaking the Cycle

Terry Solley was fourteen when his father put a pistol in his hand and took him on their first armed robbery.[5]

By eighteen, he was serving an eleven-year sentence for multiple offenses. He was released when he was twenty-nine and stayed out for just over a year before he and his father were arrested again for robbing a Wells Fargo bank. Terry spent seventeen more years in prison, totaling twenty-eight years behind bars.

During Terry's first time in prison, he joined a gang and rose through the ranks. He spent eight and a half years in solitary confinement for threatening the order and safety of the institution. During that time, he spent twenty-three hours a day alone, locked in his cell.

Though Terry had gone to church as a child, that stopped when he started robbing banks. However, when he was in solitary awaiting trial for his second prison term, God captured his attention. At the time, Terry understood the gospel and would have said, "Jesus is my Savior." But when visitors entered the unit and shared the gospel, he realized he didn't just need a Savior—he needed a Lord. He surrendered his life to Christ.

After sentencing, it took two and a half more years before Terry was moved from solitary into the general prison population. This transfer placed him directly into the disciple-making system of the prison seminary, pioneered by outsider Don Waybright and insider David Ludwick. Terry became involved and immediately translated his learning into action. He demonstrated his transformation by faithfully sharing the gospel, and soon, disciples were meeting in each day room in the prison. Terry proved he was ready to handle the extreme pressure and volatile environment of one of the state's most critical mission fields.

In 2020, Terry was transferred from Darrington to serve in the Polunsky Death Row unit, staying with the condemned men right up until their final walks.

A prisoner named Anibal, on death row for twenty-three years for murdering another inmate, recognized Terry from twenty years earlier when they were in rival gangs. Stunned by the radical change in Terry, Anibal committed his life to Christ and became a "person of peace," through whom the gospel spread to other inmates.

Death row is divided into sections where fourteen men live together in separate cells but share the same day room. Thanks to the efforts of Terry and inmate Troop Foster, churches now meet every day in six sections of death row.

Terry explains the power of this approach: "In prison, church is a group of four or five men sitting around the table, studying the Word of God, worshipping together, taking communion together, holding each other accountable, modeling what following Jesus looks like." He emphasizes that the church's effectiveness stems from the men leading it themselves, sharpening and discipling one another. This strategy has led to disciples in forty-two of the 104 prisons in Texas.

"If a man comes to Christ, his relational world is affected," Terry says, describing the ripple effect. "Prison gives you a concept of what it means to be a man, but the Bible offers a completely different perspective. We give men the opportunity to live their lives as men of God inside prison. We have men who surrender their lives to the Lord in prison, and their wives and children see the difference. They come to the Lord, and they join the Christian community on the outside."

On a personal note, Terry recalls that his own father, who was in the seminary program at Darrington, surrendered his life to the Lord: "My father watched me and saw a different son than the one he raised. My dad gave his life to the Lord because he saw the positive change in me. He was sixty-three years old. Shortly after, he died of stage four lung cancer."

Terry is now out of prison and supports long-term offenders as they reenter society. His mission is clear: "We want these men to take the gospel back into the prisons and to the streets. We want them to break the generational cycle," he says.

That passion is driven by his own experience: "I broke my wife's heart when I left her alone with our five-month-old daughter. Other men have left their wives brokenhearted and their children without a father. The Lord has changed me; he reconciled my family, and he restored the relationship with my daughter. Every time I think of her, it motivates me to do what I do. I don't want another wife heartbroken. I don't want another child to be raised without their father."

Troop Foster: From Hate to Hope

Troop Foster, a pioneer of the movement in Darrington, was transferred with Terry to work on death row.[6] "Most of my life has been a calamity of drug addiction and alcoholism, gangs and prison," he admits. "I was a white supremacist. My gang was the Aryan Brotherhood." Every time he was released from prison, Troop tried to build a life without God, but he always returned to drugs. His desperate parents and wife would ask, "Why do you come out, climb back up the mountain, then jump back into the grave?" He had no answer.

When Troop committed a capital offense, two jurors blocked the death penalty, and the judge sentenced him to forty years. He'll be seventy-seven when he's first eligible for parole. Troop spent eight years in solitary for joining the Aryan Brotherhood. Each day, he was allowed one hour in the day room, alone. While incarcerated, he lost two close family members: His mother died, followed by his teenage son. Alone in the world, Troop felt there was no reason to keep going. He considered suicide, but he remembered Jesus from his youth. Though his parents never went to church, they had sent him. Alone in his cell, he finally surrendered. He knelt and prayed a simple, desperate prayer: "God, you're going to have to do this. I can't do it. If you're real, show me."

As he lay back in his bunk, he knew something had shifted: "I felt God say, 'You've been claiming you know me for a long time, but you ain't never followed me.'" He got up and started throwing sin out—shoving dozens of pornographic magazines out under his door. Having finally surrendered, he began reading God's Word, and his life changed. His hunger for drugs vanished, and he realized, "All my life, I'd been missing a relationship with my Creator."

To get out of solitary, Troop had to go through the GRAD program, but the waiting list was six years long. During that wait, he was diagnosed with stage four cancer. He spent a year in the prison hospital, his weight dropping to 120 pounds (55 kg), and as the cancer spread, he was moved to hospice care.

Cancer didn't shake Troop. Despite struggling with chemotherapy, daily sickness, losing his hair, and watching his teeth fall out, he was at peace for the first time in his life. He was ready to go and be with Jesus, but his praying grandmother intervened: "You're not going to quit! I don't care what the doctor said. You're going to go back and get treatment and let Jesus do what Jesus does!"

Troop listened to his grandmother. "When my cancer was cured, I wasn't happy," he recalls. "I told God, I don't deserve this! Why not heal an innocent child instead of me?"

Once Troop had completed the GRAD program, he was released back into prison life after eight years in solitary. "It was hard," he admits. "In solitary, I felt like Jonah in the belly of a whale. When the whale finally spat me out, I had some choices to make." He lacked knowledge of what it meant to follow God and what his plan was for his life. "I didn't know that God wanted me to tell others about him."

Then he heard about the seminary starting at Darrington. It felt like an answer to prayer. Though he had been a poor high school student, God gave Troop a desire to study, and he earned good grades at seminary. "God was molding and shaping me. He gave me a group of brothers who invested in me. They loved me—something I'd never experienced in my life. I knew what I wanted to do. God was leading me back to where I'd come from."

Three years later, Troop was among the first field ministers assigned to the guys in solitary: the troublemakers, the gang leaders, the drug dealers, the violent men. Just like he had once been. He quickly focused on Pancho, a member of the Mesquite Mafia, in prison for murder and in solitary for seventeen years. At first, Pancho showed no interest, but then Troop saw him reading his Bible. Though he was still a gang member, Pancho asked for baptism and was baptized in chains. Others would ask Troop how Pancho could be a gang member and a follower of Christ. "Life in the gang was all Pancho knew," Troop explains. "His uncles, brothers, and cousins were all gang members. Walking away means losing everybody. But I knew it was only a matter of time before Pancho would leave the gang." Six months later, that time arrived.

Pancho is now in the GRAD program, learning how to share his faith and make disciples. "Men like Pancho were led into the gangs, so someone must lead them out," Troop says. "That requires both respect and challenge."

He asks men like Pancho several core questions:

- Why are you tied to something that's drowning you?
- Why are you serving this gang family instead of your family?
- Would you want your daughter to date a gang member?
- Do you want your son to become a gang member?

Troop urges them to raise their children in Christ. He gets to watch men become free as they surrender their lives to the Lord and immediately start making disciples right where they are.

When Terry and Troop began ministering on death row, the men in solitary weren't allowed to leave their cells; it was too dangerous. So Terry and Troop set up outside their cells and taught them how to follow Jesus. They'd do church with each inmate standing behind their steel bars, shouting to participate. The men learned to sing, eventually filling their days with worship and song. They established a form of church that now meets daily.

Troop remembers one prisoner named Tracy Beattie, who was deeply disturbed. He would sit in his cell for hours talking to someone who wasn't there, and he'd scream at the other inmates. Guards and prisoners hated him because he was always causing trouble and refused to shower. "We'd stand outside his cell, and sometimes he'd talk, sometimes he'd just yell at us," Troop recalls.

When Tracy received his execution date, he was moved to a section where he could be watched around the clock. The prisoners in that unit, having previously endured Tracy's screaming and lack of hygiene, expected the worst.

There were two disciples in the section, also waiting for their executions. Troop asked the officials to put Tracy between them, and the two agreed to "love on him." They began sharing their food and initiating conversations. Every time Tracy started talking to himself, one of them would call out, "Who you talking to, bro?" and start a conversation.

God did a miracle. Tracy committed his life to Christ and was soon singing worship songs in the day room. Terry Solley baptized him on a Sunday; he was executed the following Tuesday. Tracy Beattie, once known as a murderer and "crazy man," went to his execution singing "Amazing Grace."

The Humility and Glory of God

On death row, I saw the life and love of God on display in the darkest of places. Movements rely on strategies and methods, but they are nothing without the life that Christ brings. They are the cumulative result of countless prodigals coming home to the Father and learning his ways.

In the Western world, there are few multiplying movements of disciples and churches. The Texas prison movement is the best example I know. It reveals the humility of God that he chooses the foolish to reveal his glory to the wise.

What God can do within the walls of death row, he can do anywhere.

Reflect and Act

While this story is unique, its lessons are universal. This isn't just a prison story. It's a story about God and how he works in the world. To apply these lessons, this section challenges you to reflect on the movement dynamics presented in the story and to live them out in your own context.

As you reflect, remember the three essentials of a multiplying movement:

A movement's *Identity* mirrors the life and ministry of Jesus: obedient to the Word, dependent on the Holy Spirit, and faithful to the mission.

A movement's *Strategy* provides a clear path for expressing *Identity* in action—entering, gospeling, discipling, forming churches, and multiplying leaders.

A movement's *Methods* serve its *Strategy* and must be simple, effective, and contagious.

Movement Dynamics

Movements are a work of God. The work in Texas was initiated by a just and loving God who forgave these men through Christ—a condemned criminal who bore their sin. The movement's *Identity* isn't based on prison culture but is shaped by God's living Word and his power through the Holy Spirit. These men were at the end of their rope, facing long sentences or execution. They had failed their loved ones and were trapped in a life of crime and violence. They wanted a way out—not cheap forgiveness but grace that changes everything.

Movements are sustained by insider and outsider leadership. A traditional prison ministry asks, *What can we (outsiders) do to serve prisoners (insiders)?* A movement approach asks, *How can the Word and the Spirit work through these insiders to reach their world?* God brought Don Waybright, an outsider, into Darrington Prison with a simple, biblical, and replicable strategy. God selected David Ludwick, as an insider, to carry out the strategy. Speaking of David, Don says, "He's the pioneer and visionary. He used his role as a field minister to birth a movement. He's broken through barriers and taken others with him. He's united the men around the core missionary task. He's released authority and responsibility to others. Ludwick has been the one developing the curriculum, creating the systems, breaking through the barriers, and figuring things out. He knows how to navigate the political realities within a prison system for the good of the movement." Insiders were given authority and responsibility. Soon, the insiders were training and coaching and relating to the prison authorities.

***Movements are supported by a clear* Strategy *and simple* Methods.** Don Waybright brought the 4-Fields *Strategy* of entering, gospeling, discipling, forming churches, and multiplying leaders. Simple *Methods* were applied to each step, ensuring the newest disciples knew what to do and how to do it.

Movements practice the priesthood of every disciple. The prisoners joined God in his work of redemption, becoming ministers of the gospel. They are "a chosen people, a royal priesthood, a holy nation, God's special possession" (1 Peter 2:9), called out of darkness to declare his praises.

A traditional ministry meets the needs of prisoners. But a movement goes further, equipping and challenging prisoners to make disciples and establish churches themselves. The focus shifts from passive recipient to active participant.

Movements multiply through every available channel. They leveraged strategic partnerships (such as the seminary program and transfers) to train disciple makers and accelerate expansion, but the movement was not dependent on official recognition. The movement multiplied through two parallel tracks: Trained field ministers were strategically transferred to start groups in other prisons, while the message simultaneously spread naturally from day room to day room and from prisoners to their families.

Applying the Pattern

Reflect

These men knew they were lost, and their only hope was God revealed in Jesus Christ. The living God is at the heart of this movement, shaping its *Identity*. His Word goes out in the power of the Spirit, and the fruit is disciples and churches to his glory.

Act

Read through the passages below and note how the interplay of the Word, the Spirit, and the core missionary task forms the movement's *Identity*.

- Luke 3:21–23; 4:1–14
- Luke 24:36–49

What needs to change in your understanding and practice to align with the movement of God?

____

____

____

____

____

2

Victory Through Tears

Laos

They triumphed over him by the blood of the Lamb and by the word of their testimony; they did not love their lives so much as to shrink from death.

REVELATION 12:11

After the 1975 Communist revolution in Laos, Noy, a promising student, was sent to study in Moscow. While there, he learned Russian, completed his degree, and found Christ through a campus ministry. He returned home and married Chantha. Together, they began to plant a church.

Their work drew the authorities' attention. The Communists arrested Noy and charged him with "fomenting social division." They offered him an immediate release, on one condition: "Stop preaching, and you can go home; otherwise, we'll keep you here forever." But Noy stood firm, refusing their demand.

Chantha was forbidden to see Noy for six months. Despite this, Noy managed to send her a single message: "Whatever happens in life or death, keep guiding believers to worship and serve God." Soon, Lao, Chinese, and Vietnamese released prisoners started arriving at Chantha's home, bringing astonishing news: They had put their faith in Christ through Noy's witness in prison. Stunned, Chantha realized Noy's ministry had continued even in chains.

After two and a half years, Chantha was finally told to collect her husband. Noy was to be released on probation, but the prison officials demanded he sign a statement promising to stop sharing the gospel. Noy refused the condition, yet remarkably, they released him anyway.

Free from jail, Noy moved his young family to an unreached province. For almost a decade (1996–2005), he worked relentlessly, entering unreached villages, sharing the gospel, training new disciples, and planting churches. He returned to strengthen them and develop leaders, and as the number of disciples climbed to over three thousand, the sharp increase drew renewed attention from the State. However, the threat of prison did not stop Noy. Though the police warned him that he was on a watch list, he remained resolute, telling friends, "One day, my body will be found alongside the road. It's because so many are coming to know Jesus."

During the Christmas season in December 2005, Noy was traveling between churches, while Chantha remained at home caring for their five children. After one service, as the church shared a Christmas meal, two men arrived on motorbikes. They sat either side of Noy and insisted he come with them, claiming they had "work to do." Though the believers were worried, Noy comforted them, assuring them he would be okay, and agreed to go. As the two men started their motorbikes, Noy got on the back of one, and the three men vanished.

The concerned believers immediately began a search. Near the church, where the road cut through the dense jungle, Noy's body was found. He had been brutally murdered.

The Day Division Died

Distraught, Chantha decided that Noy must have a public funeral in Vientiane, the national capital. She wanted the authorities to see that Christ's followers were not intimidated. Hundreds gathered to honor Noy's sacrifice and support his family.

Peter, a longtime worker among the Lao people, attended the funeral and recalls the deep division within the Lao Christian community at that time: "The National Registered church and the unregistered house churches were separate streams. Both were faithful followers of the Lord, but they did not trust each other. Noy was one of the few whom both sides trusted." Noy's funeral marked the first time leaders from both groups had come together in years. "As they prayed and mourned for Noy, they resolved that their divisions must end," Peter says.

This marked a clear turning point in Lao church history, as registered and unregistered church leaders began to trust one another. "It changed everything," Peter concludes. A shared vision for unity and multiplication took root, preparing the way for the movement that would follow.

From Widow to Movement Leader

Meanwhile, everything was shifting for Chantha. Until Noy's death, she had been a schoolteacher who supported her husband's ministry. "I despaired when my husband died," she admits. "I said, 'Lord, take me, too. I can't go on.'"

Unsure what to do, she prayed and fasted for fifteen days. She cried out to the Lord, and he answered. "I read John 15 about remaining in Christ and bearing much fruit. Then God told me, 'Whatever you do, whether you're sleeping, waking, or eating, you're meant to go and revive the church.'" God told her to strengthen the churches her husband had started. "Noy's calling became my calling," she says. "God gave Noy the vision for multiplying disciples, churches, and leaders throughout the province. Now that vision has become a reality as I trusted and served God despite the obstacles." When the believers saw her strength, they were inspired and eager to serve God alongside her.

Chantha left her government job as a teacher to continue Noy's ministry. "We've grown from three thousand disciples to over ten thousand in fifty-six churches," she notes. "God has done it. God has ordained it." Now, teams of Lao workers are crossing into neighboring countries. "Some have been arrested and beaten, but they still have faith. They are pressing on." The vision God shared with her husband continues through her, their now-adult children, and all the disciples.

Coffee in Bangkok

In a café in Bangkok, Thailand, I sat down with two church-planting catalysts among the Lao people: Peter, the veteran worker who had attended Noy's funeral, and John, a Lao American. I wanted to understand how this movement emerged and how it spread.

Peter: Outsider to Insider

Peter's involvement began in the 1990s. Arriving as an outsider with no local connections, he searched for a "family of peace"—a God-prepared household open to the gospel and connected to their community. While working on a development project, Peter met Daw, a respected leader in his clan. Peter recognized Daw as the person of peace he was looking for and patiently waited for the right moment to share the gospel.

One evening, Peter arrived at Daw's small house and found him engaged in a Khmu sword dance, which was part of a demon ceremony. A crowd of about twenty people had gathered inside. Peter poked his head in, acknowledged the ceremony, and told Daw he would wait outside.

Once Daw had finished the ceremony, he invited Peter in. An opportunity immediately presented itself when one of the village elders spoke up, asking, "The government tells us Jesus is the enemy of the State. Why are they so worried about him? Who is this Jesus?"

Over the next hour, Peter shared the gospel, answering numerous questions from many of those present. Though Daw was secretly interested, he remained notably quiet throughout the discussion.

After that evening, Daw and Peter met several more times. Peter challenged Daw to respond to God's invitation, and Daw eventually surrendered to Christ. The pair continued to meet secretly three to five times a week to read the Bible, and Daw learned how to follow Jesus and make disciples. He quit drinking and stopped beating his wife. His dramatic transformation not only drew the attention of his wife but also the entire village.

Peter trained Daw to share his faith, and Daw then led his family to Christ. As Daw shared everything he learned with others, a church of forty baptized disciples was born, with Daw as its leader.

The rapid rise of the new church troubled the authorities. The local governor responded by having the village surrounded by armed soldiers, demanding that the believers renounce their faith. They arrested seven church leaders, who spent up to six months in jail. The persecution forced all church activity—from evangelism to training and gathering—underground. If caught, Christians faced worse consequences than convicted drug dealers. Peter remembers, "We did our best work after dark."

Peter trained local believers across four provinces on how to find families of peace, make disciples, and plant churches.

By 2006, the disciples had baptized thousands of new believers across four streams of multiplying churches. Despite this growth, less than 1 percent of Laos's population was Christian, and over a hundred people groups still hadn't heard the gospel.

The cost of faithfulness rose. Hundreds of believers were jailed, and six disciples were murdered, including Daw, his wife, and their six-year-old son. Their bodies were never found. Though such devastating events tested the burgeoning movement, they did not stop the growth. The disciples bravely carried the vision forward.

John: Finding Timeo

In 2007, John moved from America to Laos and started a water filtration business that helped rural communities. But his main goal was to disciple a new generation of Lao believers. Guided by Peter, John dedicated himself to mentoring young men. Timeo was one of them. "He was a faithful, humble man who wasn't motivated by money," John says. "Others came and went, but Timeo stayed."

In 2012, John transitioned from managing the business to full-time disciple making. He asked Timeo to join him as a pioneer, offering him a choice: "This new work won't be easy. You'll be persecuted, even arrested. You'll have less money, less recognition—but you'll make disciples of your people."

Timeo accepted the challenge, and they formed an apostolic team with a few interns and families. John moved just across the border to Thailand, where he could mobilize short-term teams and coach Timeo remotely. Over the next four years, they led over forty teams into the villages of Laos on motorbikes, riding thousands of miles and prayer-walking in over two hundred villages. Along the way, they found people of peace, witnessed miraculous healings, and saw entire families come to faith.

By 2015, hundreds had been baptized and dozens of churches planted. And through the faith of these new disciples, the gospel began to spread to unreached people groups. The following year, John returned to Laos to stay close to Timeo and the growing movement.

In 2016, John, Timeo, Peter, and others met with leaders of the country's main evangelical denomination. The denominational leadership, frustrated by the limited results from their traditional seminary model, proved receptive to new ideas. The three men shared what God was doing through simple, biblical discipleship and church multiplication and explained why preserving an indigenous movement was crucial.

In a monumental breakthrough, the denomination's president, a respected seventy-eight-year-old church patriarch, publicly committed his remaining years to multiplying churches among every people group in Laos. "From that moment, he treated me like a son," John recalls. "He worked closely with us for the next five years until he died in 2022." To those among the established denominational leaders and pastors who resisted the change, the denominational president was clear: "We *are* going to do this."

This shift opened the door for John and Timeo to train across the denomination with the full support and involvement of its president. From 2017 to 2018, they crisscrossed the country, secretly training thousands. Apostolic pioneers emerged, tasked with establishing apostolic bands targeting unreached people groups.

By 2019, the new disciples had established second- and third-generation churches. The following year, they started fourth-generation churches. What the Lao disciples lacked in formal training, they made up for in zeal. Their burning commitment and simple, reproducible methods enabled the gospel to cross cultural and language barriers.

Since 2017, the movement has baptized over fifty thousand

new disciples and established 1,200 churches. This rapid growth follows decades of sowing. In 1990, Christians accounted for 0.2 percent of Laos's population. By 2024, that percentage had increased fifteenfold to roughly 3 percent. Streams of fourth-generation churches are now active in ten of the eighteen provinces, engaging over one hundred unreached people groups, mostly animists.

Jai: Teachable and Unstoppable

Jai was one of the apostolic pioneers sent out by his denomination in 2017 to start a movement of disciples and churches. John and Timeo trained him in the 4-Fields strategy,[1] which helped Jai to equip new believers to evangelize and to give them authority to baptize and make disciples. He learned how to help disciples recognize the traits of healthy churches (Acts 2:36–47) and how to track and evaluate the generations of new churches.[2]

Within his first year, Jai gained 474 disciples and established new churches across thirty-eight villages. This success quickly attracted the attention of the police, who arrested him. He was locked up for one year and twenty-four days. (Jai is precise about the twenty-four days!) Every week, his wife, Sawan, would take the long bus ride to visit him in prison and bring food.

Even behind bars, Jai was unstoppable. He led eleven prisoners to Christ and formed a church.

Before his release, the officials issued a threat: "Next time, you won't go to jail. You'll go on a list"—a clear warning that if Jai continued to spread the gospel, they would have him killed.

To support his family, Jai now farms rice and keeps chickens, ducks, and two cows. When he's not working his physical fields, he takes the gospel into unreached spiritual fields. He casts out demons, heals the sick, makes disciples, plants churches, and develops leaders. Thousands have turned to Christ, and they have formed hundreds of churches.

John describes Jai as "teachable and unstoppable." He continues, "He doesn't love money. He lives simply. He'll hike over a mountain, sleep on hard floors, eat what he is offered, so that he can share the gospel and form a new group of disciples."

Over a meal in Bangkok, Jai told me he wants to reach his people group of 160,000, 1,500 of whom are already following Christ. Despite the authorities' death threats, he remains determined. He won't stop.

Keeping Track

Since 2017, the movement has tracked its progress. They know how often the gospel is shared; they count newly baptized disciples, new discipleship groups, and new churches; and they also track the number of workers they train.

Laos: 2017–2024

	2017–2018	2019	2020	2021	2022	2023	2024	Total
Training Events	86	82	176	279	192	207	243	1,265
Leaders Trained	1,940	2,693	2,450	6,685	1,853	1,944	2,397	19,962
Gospel Presentations	31,648	30,608	27,289	42,547	122,053	151,288	242,488	647,921
Baptisms	3,926	3,826	2,279	3,955	10,333	8,532	6,876	39,727
New Groups	1,332	673	1,032	180	176	312	441	4,146
New Churches	133	503	227	61	144	131	120	1,319

Between 2017 and 2024, they trained and mobilized nearly twenty thousand believers to share the gospel and make disciples at over one thousand events. Over the past seven years, these disciples have shared the gospel almost 650,000 times, reaching about one in ten people, resulting in nearly forty thousand new baptized disciples. They have started over four thousand discovery and discipleship groups and established 1,319 new churches.

There is a continuous thread running through this strategy, connecting each part of their plan:

1. Casting a vision to reach every people group and every place
2. Training disciples to share the gospel and make disciples
3. Forming new groups centered on God's Word, learning to follow Christ
4. Ensuring discipleship groups develop into healthy churches that reproduce workers, disciples, and churches
5. Training and coaching leaders who make disciples and plant churches

These Lao disciples focus on outcomes they *can* control rather than ones they *can't*:

- They *can't* determine how many people come to faith, but they *can* decide how many disciples they train and with whom they share the gospel.
- They *can't* control who responds to a gospel presentation, but they *can* control whether their gospel tool is simple, biblical, and reproducible, so new disciples can immediately share it with their loved ones.
- They *can't* control whether new believers continue to grow in Christ, but they *can* form new disciples into

> obedience-based groups using a simple method for reading the Scriptures and following Christ together.
>
> - They *can't* control how many churches they start, but they *can* implement a simple pattern of church life based on Acts 2:36–47, which equips discipleship groups to become healthy churches.

They are faithful stewards of the life that only God can give through Christ, and their stewardship is marked by disciplined accountability and evaluation. To ensure the movement is not just growing wide but deep and reproducible, they employ a diagnostic tool known as the 7 Phases of a Church Planting Movement.

7 Phases of a Church Planting Movement[3]

1 Adoption	2 Gospel	3 Disciples	4 Church (1st Gen)	5 Churches Reproducing (2nd Gen)	6 Churches Multiplying (4th Gen)	7 Sustained Movement
A team has access and is implementing a church-planting strategy among this people group.	Workers sharing the gospel with the intention of planting churches.	People responding with repentance and faith expressed in baptism.	Indigenous churches worshipping God and obeying his Word. Local leaders emerging.	Indigenous churches sending workers to plant churches. 2nd-generation churches.	4th-generation churches. Authority passes from generation to generation.	Four streams of 4th-generation churches.

I've seen the maps they've drawn for each region, where local teams assess and color-code areas to identify progress, recognize the gaps, and plan for multiplication.

In 2023, with generations of churches across ten provinces, the movement entered a new phase. Timeo and local teams continue to coach dozens of apostolic bands, focusing on reaching every province. In 2024, John and his family relocated and took on a regional role across Asia.

An Eternal Reward

I've sat with those who bear the scars and stories of this movement. I listened as Peter recounted Daw, the first man of peace—how the gospel transformed his life, how he led others in faith, and how he and his family were martyred for refusing to remain silent. They will receive an eternal reward for their suffering.

I cried with Chantha as she described Noy—how he was taken from her, and how his death broke down the walls between the registered and underground churches. Chantha embodies the heart of this movement of God among the Lao, a movement with its sights set on the nations. She shares that heart with thousands of ordinary disciples.

The martyrs were the beginning of a multiplying movement that continues to bear fruit in every province and beyond borders.

Jesus taught that unless a grain of wheat falls to the ground and dies, it remains only a single seed. But if it dies, it will produce much fruit (John 12:24). The Lao disciples have learned this lesson. They have all been touched by the deaths of the martyrs. They understand the risks they take and the price they pay. The fruit is undeniable. Lao disciples are now crossing borders as missionary multipliers, and the national church has cast a bold vision: to see 10 percent of the country reached by 2030.

Reflect and Act

While this story is rooted in the rice fields and jungles of Laos, it carries universal lessons. This isn't just a story of martyrdom and endurance; it's a powerful demonstration of God turning a student, a farmer, and a widow into catalysts for a nationwide movement. To apply these lessons, this section challenges you to reflect on the movement dynamics presented in the story and to live them out.

As you reflect, remember the three essentials of a multiplying movement:

A movement's *Identity* mirrors the life and ministry of Jesus: obedient to the Word, dependent on the Holy Spirit, and faithful to the mission.

A movement's *Strategy* provides a clear path for expressing *Identity* in action—entering, gospeling, discipling, forming churches, and multiplying leaders.

A movement's *Methods* serve its *Strategy* and must be simple, effective, and contagious.

Movement Dynamics

Movements expect suffering. Leaders are jailed, and if they keep talking about Jesus, some of them may die. A wife may become widowed; children may lose their father. Yet, the gospel still advances. This was the case at Noy's funeral, where God's people came together in love and were determined to reach their nation. Through faithful suffering, they overcame the Enemy's attack.

Movements look for God-prepared people. Peter entered an unreached field, seeking out God-prepared people. He found Daw. Even before Daw became a disciple, he was inviting others to come and hear. Daw welcomed the messenger, the message, and embraced the mission. He was a person of peace.

Movements train insiders. Once Daw, an insider, came to Christ, Peter's strategy was to teach him how to reach his own people. The key to a movement is insiders like Daw, Noy, Chantha, Jai, and Timeo, who serve as the disciple makers and church planters. How you make the next disciple doesn't guarantee a movement, but it determines whether a movement can happen.

Movements value character. As a movement grows, gifted leaders emerge who may be tempted by outside funding. Because movements value character, they do not promote leaders who are lovers of money. This standard is evident in the lives of key pioneers. Jai chose to live simply—sleeping on rough floors and eating what he was offered—and Timeo chose hardship and persecution over money and recognition.

Movements face competing agendas. Peter and John shared with me two significant challenges the emerging movement faced. These obstacles—rivalry for leaders and traditional institutional influences—are universal to movements.

- *Rivalry for leaders*: Other Christian groups attracted movement pioneers with offers of salaries, advanced education, and stable positions. They introduced competing philosophies of ministry that weakened an indigenous movement. Some of the top leaders were lured away. Some streams of the movement plateaued.
- *The influence of a traditional denomination*: Centralized seminary programs risked disrupting the indigenous movement by enforcing a more rigid approach to multiplying disciples and churches.

They overcame these challenges by remaining true to their *Identity*, *Strategy*, and *Methods*. Meanwhile, God brought deep change in the denomination through Noy's martyrdom and the spiritual authority of the denomination's president.

Movements go after both depth AND breadth. This movement multiplied rapidly at times, but those breakthroughs were preceded by a long, difficult season in which persecution served as preparation, deepening and forging their *Identity*. The movement also grew in effectiveness as they consistently applied the *Strategy* of a multiplying movement. They used simple *Methods* to spread the gospel, make disciples, form churches, and multiply leaders.

Movements turn vision into action. It's one thing to aspire to reach a nation and set ambitious goals; it's another to turn that vision into tangible results. They knew who they were and what to do. They had an effective strategy and proven methods.

Applying the Pattern

Reflect

These Lao disciples are a persecuted people most of the world knows nothing about. We may be tempted to see them as victims. Yet God has chosen them in their weakness to reveal his glory. When we feel weak and overwhelmed with the challenge of reaching our world, remember these saints, these chosen ones, these royal priests, chosen to suffer for the name of Jesus, chosen to multiply disciples and churches. Everywhere.

Act

Read Luke 10:1–11.

- When Jesus sends his disciples out, what does he tell them to do?
- What does he tell them not to do?
- What specific actions will you take to follow this pattern today?
- How will you search for and engage with God-prepared people of peace?

____

____

____

____

3

Out of the Classroom, Into the Field

Indonesia

"Come, follow me," Jesus said, "and I will send you out to fish for people."

MATTHEW 4:19

Zak grew up in a Christian home in Indonesia but drifted from his parents' faith. He began using and selling drugs, which eventually led to a jail cell. It was behind bars that he reencountered the gospel. Weekly visits from Christians repeated the message he'd heard for years, but for the first time, he understood it. Overwhelmed by God's grace, Zak repented and committed his life to Christ. While still in jail, Zak felt a growing call to reach Muslims.

After he was released, he enrolled in seminary and went out daily to engage Muslims and share the gospel.

It was at seminary that Zak met Mike, an American missionary, who had spent his early years in Indonesia doing what missionaries traditionally do—teaching in a seminary and strengthening existing churches. Yet Mike grew troubled by the gap between his experience and the Great Commission's calling. God had unsettled him. Mike decided to make a radical shift, moving "from the classroom to the field. From pulpit training to straw mat training."

In 2004, Mike took on the daunting responsibility for an unreached people group of several million Muslims. The challenge drove him to prayer and to the Scriptures as his guide for making disciples. "It was hard at first," Mike recalls. "God humbled us and showed us the simplicity of the Great Commission."

After graduating and training with Mike for four months, Zak was ready to relocate to another city. There, Zak spent eight hours every day sharing the gospel with Muslims. He took the gospel to the mosque, the marketplace, schools, and neighborhoods. Initially, there was no fruit. But Zak persevered, believing the gospel that had saved him could also save Muslims.

The Outsider–Insider Partnership

The first breakthrough came when Zak led Tamir to Christ.

Tamir was a farmer struggling to support his young family. He was so desperate, he now admits, "I would have worshipped Satan if it had helped." When he first heard about Jesus through Zak, his initial thought was, *Maybe if I get close to Jesus, my prayers will be answered.*

Every Wednesday, Tamir walked for hours to meet with Zak and study the Bible. He set out hoping to solve his financial problems. He stayed because the gospel did its transformative work. As Tamir read the story of Adam and Eve, he recognized his own sin had separated him from God. Zak explained that God had bridged that gap through Jesus and that he offered Tamir forgiveness and restored relationship—a truth Islam had not taught him. He turned to Christ, and Zak baptized him. Tamir's transformation was clear. His family saw it, and he began to bring them to Christ: his wife, children, parents, parents-in-law, and his brothers and sisters. Soon, he was leading his friends and neighbors to Christ as well.

This sudden surge of new believers drew the attention of the local Imams, who complained to the police. Tamir was arrested and interrogated. The officers threatened to burn his house and warned that he could face fifteen years in jail. His children were bullied at school. But Tamir stood firm and would not stop sharing the gospel. His faithful witness eventually led two officers to put their faith in Christ.

Zak taught Tamir how to read the Bible and make disciples. Following a 3-Thirds pattern, they read the passage, then asked:[1]

- What is this story or passage about?
- What do you learn about God?
- What is the most interesting part?
- Why is this still relevant?
- What must we do to obey?
- With whom will you share this?

Through Zak's training and coaching, Tamir, the bankrupt farmer, became Tamir, the movement catalyst. Zak showed Tamir how to make disciples with a method called MAWL:

- *Model*: Show them how to do it.
- *Assist*: Help them do it.
- *Watch*: Provide feedback.
- *Launch*: They've got it.

Two decades later, Tamir still shares his faith with five to ten people daily. He has followed the model Zak provided, training numerous disciples and leaders—so many that he's lost count.

Getting to Church

In 2005, Zak's focus was on evangelism and making disciples who make disciples. He saw success, but a critical piece was missing: The new disciples were not consistently establishing and reproducing churches with a healthy discipleship ethos.

Zak and Mike addressed this by creating resources to train disciples and emerging leaders that stressed the importance of obeying the Great Commission as a continuous process, emphasizing connection to Christ and obedience to the Commission. They taught that the Great Commission doesn't end with evangelism; it is a continuous process of making disciples throughout the whole world.

Mike defines the heart of the Great Commission: "Make disciples of all the *ethne* (every people group)," supported by two assurances: Jesus' authority and presence. The essential tasks are "Go, baptize, and teach them to obey."

Zak explains their methodology: "We lead people to faith, baptize them, and teach them to start a group of disciples that becomes a church. When those disciples and churches reproduce generations, a movement is born."

The resources Zac and Mike developed to support this vision guide believers through a discipleship plan that empowers them to obey everything Scripture expects of disciples. A crucial part of their training involves a clear pathway to establishing thriving churches. Over the years, they have honed and refined this pathway to make it as simple, understandable, and repeatable as possible. As a result, churches are now consistently multiplying to the fourth generation and beyond. Multiple streams of reproducing disciples and churches have emerged across Indonesia, especially among hard-to-reach, unreached people groups.

Zak shares the example of Yusuf, a young man in his

mid-twenties, who was challenged by a coworker: "'If you obey all the commands of Scripture, I'll mentor you.'" He agreed and was baptized. Just four months later, Yusuf had led three people to faith. One of them, Zakir, started a church in his home and baptized two others. Following the model, each of the new disciples began a church in their home while Yusuf discipled them. Three years later, Yusuf's initial disciple making had resulted in a thousand baptized believers and forty new churches.

Field-Driven Learning

Between 2005 and 2009, Zak and Mike focused on developing multiple streams of reproducing disciples and churches. This vision generated the necessary tension and energy to fuel their learning. As they trained emerging leaders, they constantly tested solutions and reviewed the results.

Their methodology was grounded in three critical sources of guidance:

- *The Scriptures*: The Bible served as their authority for both their theology and their practices in the field. They studied the Scriptures, seeking insights to solve practical problems in multiplying disciples and churches.
- *Action and reflection*: With the Bible in their hands, they engaged in the work, expecting the Holy Spirit to lead, guide, and shape the outcomes. Zak and his leaders were out eight hours each day, sharing the gospel, making disciples, and forming churches. Every week, workers reported in and evaluated their progress.
- *Best practices*: They learned from case studies in other fields and carefully applied the lessons. This was a dynamic process of trial and error, experiment, and evaluation. As

they identified key lessons, they revised the curriculum for workers, providing step-by-step guides for evangelism, discipleship, church planting, and leadership training.

At one point, Zak and Mike recognized a critical hindrance to the movement's growth: They were doing too much of the leading and training themselves, fostering dependence rather than independence. For example, leaders continued to bring new disciples to Zak for baptism, which was unsustainable if the movement was to grow. Zak and Mike read the New Testament with fresh eyes and discovered that any disciple could baptize and celebrate the Lord's Supper. Jesus has given every disciple the authority to obey his command to make disciples, not just select leaders.

Zak and Mike revised their curriculum to integrate this theological insight, along with other necessary changes identified through their ongoing health and growth assessments. After updating the training, they performed field tests of the adapted methods. This commitment to continuous, field-driven learning paid off: By 2015, they had leaders who were multiplying churches to fifteen generations, mainly in Central Java.

With a field-tested strategy in place, they started planting churches throughout the rest of Indonesia by training and sending workers. Team members were deployed to the provinces of Aceh, Medan, Java, Sumatra, Sulawesi, and Jakarta. Leveraging the close linguistic ties between Indonesian and Malay, they also sent short-term teams to work among Malay speakers in Malaysia, Thailand, Singapore, and Brunei.

Jakarta

After years of multiplying in Central Java, Zak had Jakarta, the nation's capital, on his heart. The challenge was immense: to establish the same principles in a megacity of 30 million people. He was looking for someone to pioneer the work. God reminded him of Usman, a believer and a business leader in the city who grew up with Zak.

While Usman was riding high on his business success, Zak's priorities had shifted. Zak—the man who once saved Usman from a fight by stabbing an attacker—was now focused on serving God. He challenged Usman: "Let's reach the world with the gospel until we die!" That's all Zak wanted to talk about.

Usman was interested but didn't know how to begin. From then on, whenever Zak was in town, he would take him out, sharing the gospel and making disciples.

Zak demonstrated what to do once or twice before throwing Usman in at the deep end. On one bus ride, Usman started a conversation with a stranger but then froze, unsure of what to say next. He expected Zak to intervene, but Zak said nothing, letting Usman sit in the awkward silence.

Zak sent Usman on a ten-day trip to Malaysia to reach out to Muslim Malays. Usman returned a different man, ready to join the Jakarta team. He began going out most days, sharing the gospel and looking for God-prepared people, while running his businesses in his spare time.

Usman applied the Any-3 strategy—anyone, anywhere, anytime[2]—sharing with whomever he met. One day, he met a 4-star army general in a shopping mall. As he shared, Usman realized that this was the newly appointed Indonesian Minister for Religion!

When compared with the rapid growth seen in rural villages, progress in a city like Jakarta is slow. But so far, the teams Usman has trained have planted 250 churches, each typically averaging between four and twelve people.

A Movement Leader

Zak is clear on the vision God has given him: "Our calling is to multiply disciples and churches throughout Indonesia and Southeast Asia using simple, biblical, reproducible methods."

It's a big task. There are 250 million Malay speakers in Indonesia and Southeast Asia.[3] Zak focuses on training and mentoring local leaders and movement catalysts, ensuring they master the principles and skills that drive movements.

"Our workers don't plant churches," Zak says. "Our workers take the gospel to unreached places and peoples, then help new disciples plant churches." His team is highly committed to the cause, spending eight hours a day entering unreached communities and sharing the gospel. "They don't go home until they've shared the gospel with five to ten people."

Catalysts send in daily reports. Every week, they meet online for evaluation. Zak's maintained this disciplined approach for twelve years with his nine core leaders. None of them are paid office staff; they're all field workers. They work hard. Zak says, "They do what Mike and I did in the beginning."

Zak sets a model of dedication, which team member Tamir confirms: "Zak makes high demands of us, but he works hard. He is with us. He faces the same challenges. He's a man who depends on God." Zak powerfully demonstrated his commitment during a crisis in Brunei. After one of their teams was arrested and interrogated, he sought to dispel fear and model a way forward. Three days after his team's release, Zak flew to Brunei, knowing the police would recognize his name as the team's leader. He visited their local contacts, encouraged the team, and demonstrated that they didn't need to fear the police. As a result, teams have continued to go to the country. This bold response reflects Zak's core belief about the inevitable persecution: "That's the price we pay. We teach our disciples to suffer for Christ."

When Movements Settle Down, God Intervenes

In Acts, God disrupted Peter at Simon's house in Joppa with a vision of unclean animals (Acts 10:9–16). But it was at Cornelius's house (Acts 10:28) that Peter understood the purpose of that vision: The disciples, though given the Great Commission to go to the nations (Matthew 28:19), had neglected the Gentile mission. Their identity as a missionary movement was under threat. The Holy Spirit opened a door, and Peter was the first to walk through it, with others following.

A similar missional correction pattern occurred in the birth of this movement through Mike and Zak. God led them on a long, arduous journey of narrowing the gap between the Great Commission and their experience. Like Peter, they are exceptional individuals, but the initiative for this movement was with God. Mike and Zak were faithful to their calling. They planted and watered; God gave the growth.

Reflect and Act

While the Indonesian story is unique, its lessons on multiplication and perseverance are universal. This isn't just a mission report. It's a story about God and how he works through disciplined, reproducing movements. To apply these lessons, this section challenges you to reflect on the movement dynamics presented in the story and to live them out in your own context.

As you reflect, remember the three essentials of a multiplying movement:

A movement's *Identity* mirrors the life and ministry of Jesus: obedient to the Word, dependent on the Holy Spirit, and faithful to the mission.

A movement's *Strategy* provides a clear path for expressing *Identity* in action—entering, gospeling, discipling, forming churches, and multiplying leaders.

A movement's *Methods* serve its *Strategy* and must be simple, effective, and contagious.

Movement Dynamics

Movements have a Great Commission vision. Mike and Zak allowed the Great Commission to challenge them and their strategy, refusing to lower the vision to the level of their experience. The tension between vision and reality fueled their learning.

Movements employ field-driven learning. Their core mission was to disciple and establish churches among unreached people groups. When the gospel was advancing and leading to disciples but not healthy churches, they asked, *Why not?* This field-driven critique identified a crucial missing element in their strategy. They then focused on simplifying and communicating the way to church formation. The result was generations of churches across multiple people groups.

Movements are not dependent on any one individual, including the founders. Mike served as the outside catalyst, forming a partnership with Zak, the founder who embodied the movement's purpose and pioneered its effective strategies and methods. Their strategic goal was always to ensure the movement emerged as a cause, no longer dependent on any individual, including the founders.[4]

Applying the Pattern

Reflect

Movements know the Father's heart for a lost world. They turn a God-sized vision into action, and the learning begins. Sometimes the process takes years, but as disciples go, Jesus promises them his presence. Mike and Zak have been on this journey. They've persevered in lean times and seen the breakthroughs. They've learned the lessons, and now there's a multiplying movement that has a life of its own.

Act

- Describe your Great Commission vision for multiplying disciples and churches.
- Review your calendar for the last month. How have you grounded your vision in action?
- What do you need to do to align your life with the vision God has given you?

4

Depth *and* Breadth

India

And beginning with Moses and all the Prophets, he explained to them what was said in all the Scriptures concerning himself.

LUKE 24:27

With 1.4 billion people, thousands of languages, and massive Hindu and Muslim populations, India is a complex and challenging mission field. While the Christian presence has historically been in the south, this is now shifting as the gospel moves northward.

Cursed by the Gods

Ravi's trouble began at conception. He was conceived just eight months after his brother's birth—a narrow span that, according to superstition, had cursed him in the eyes of the gods. His mother made a desperate, failed attempt to abort him. He grew up rejected by his alcoholic father, who blamed Ravi for any and every misfortune. When a thunderstorm broke, he was sent out of the house, fearing he might attract lightning. When his father gambled and lost, Ravi was beaten.

Ravi grew up resenting his parents, drawn to crime, drugs, and alcohol from a young age. He hoped the money he brought home would win his father's acceptance, but it didn't. Toying with suicide, he was at a low point when his Christian uncle gave Ravi's father a Bible. His father never read it, but Ravi did. Through its pages, he came to know the God revealed through Jesus Christ.

When Ravi was baptized, it was his mother who beat him. His father told him, "From now on, you pay to live here." The beatings continued, but he no longer believed he was cursed. A year later, his father threw him out.

The Beginning of an Outsider–Insider Partnership

Ravi moved to the city to live with relatives and found work as a handyman. As he continued to read his Bible, he developed a strong desire to share the gospel with others. His uncle sponsored him to attend Bible college. However, as the only student from a Hindu background, he felt like an outsider. Classes were taught in English, but he only spoke Hindi, so he taught himself English by reading the English-Hindi Bible.

Eventually, Ravi moved to another Bible college, where he met Gary. Gary and his wife, Veronica, had moved from the United States to make disciples and raise their family. They were learning the language and culture, as well as how to communicate the gospel to Hindus. At the time, Gary was handing out tracts and New Testaments and showing the Jesus film.[1] He was also training and mobilizing local believers. Gary understood the principles of church planting movements, but he was still learning how to apply them.

Gary had connected with the Bible college specifically to find students who shared his drive to make disciples. Ravi immediately stood out; he was at college because he wanted to learn how to make disciples. Gary and Veronica welcomed Ravi into their home and family, and before long, Gary and Ravi started working together. They shared the gospel on the streets and in the neighborhoods, screening the Jesus film and handing out tracts and Bibles.

Although Ravi was eager to learn and do, Gary wondered at the time why God hadn't given him more workers, praying, "Lord, don't you think you could trust me with more than just one guy?" He later realized that God had answered his prayer perfectly, because the guy God gave him was more than enough. God had brought Gary, the outsider catalyst, together with Ravi, the insider apostolic pioneer.[2]

Careful Adjustments

Ravi and Gary assessed the effectiveness of their strategy and methods, concluding that a simple gospel outline might not be enough to penetrate the deeply entrenched worldview of Hindus or Muslims. Ravi himself had come to Christ only after a long search through the Scriptures, and his decision had stuck.

They also questioned the effectiveness of targeting individuals rather than entire households. This led them to develop a strategy of guiding families through a series of Bible stories, starting with Creation and ending with the new Creation in Christ. They piloted a series of thirty-five studies called *Ek Rasta* (the Way).

Every Saturday, they would lock themselves away to write the lesson for the following week. They tested the new study with households, observing how God used the lessons and adjusting them accordingly. Working eighty-hour weeks for twelve months, they oversaw the whole project—training workers, opening new households, and writing the studies. They followed up the *Ek*

Rasta series with a nine-lesson course on discipleship and church formation.

Households were turning to Christ and learning how to follow him. Growth was steady but slow. Then the breakthrough came. Ravi and Gary had a policy of working both "near and far"—with "far" sometimes meaning hundreds of miles away. It was a focus on the "far" that led them to travel out of the city in 2012 to visit a worker who had gathered a group of fifteen new believers. When Ravi and Gary asked the group about their newfound faith, their answers revealed a knowledge gap. They trusted in Jesus, but they didn't know what they believed or why.

Ravi guided them through the first seven of the thirty-five *Ek Rasta* lessons. He promised to return in four weeks and encouraged them to keep working through the studies. They proved faithful, and the group doubled in size to about thirty people. But Ravi pushed them further, urging everyone to start their own groups. He didn't expect anyone to meet the challenge. However, when he returned, 180 *Ek Rasta* groups were already meeting! On average, each person had started six groups.

To keep pace with this exponential growth, Gary and Ravi discovered the power of microSD cards. Due to limited literacy, the *Ek Rasta* lessons were initially presented in a printed storybook. However, they realized that microSD cards could store large amounts of information in text, audio, and video files. The cards cost only a few dollars, and most households have a basic phone that can read a card.

The microSD cards revolutionized the workers' approach. Now they had the confidence to go from household to household, offering a card and scheduling a return visit to discuss the studies. This technological innovation was like pouring fuel on the fire, turbocharging growth and enabling scalability. After seven years, they had a strategy and simple methods in place that catalyzed a movement of hundreds of thousands of new disciples and the establishment of tens of thousands of new churches.

I spent ten days with Ravi and Gary. We drove hundreds of miles, visiting the disciples and churches scattered throughout the region. As part of my research, I asked individuals and households, "How did the gospel come to you and your family?" Then, "How did the gospel go from you to others?"

Other times during our travels, I'd sit with Gary and Ravi in a shaded courtyard or inside, while a noisy fan struggled to keep us cool. Young children ran in and out as we drank chai—tea made by boiling buffalo milk, spices, ginger, and lots of sugar—and it was during those times that they shared the details of their strategy.

1. Entering Unreached Fields

They went to people who were far from God. Typically, these individuals were miserable and found no consolation in Hinduism. Then someone showed up at their door—a relative, a neighbor, or someone they'd never met before—sharing their story of meeting Christ and offering prayer.

As I conducted interviews, I often heard testimonies like this: "My husband was a lazy drunkard, always angry, and demons oppressed him. Our family was poor and in despair. Then two people came to our home to tell us how they met Jesus. They prayed for us. God healed one of our family members. Jesus brought peace into our home. My husband was set free. He doesn't drink anymore. He listens to me; he cares for our family and even helps with jobs around the house! He goes out to work, and now our lives are much better."

I met those formerly angry, drunkard, demon-possessed men; they had become godly men full of the life of Christ.

I also met an elderly widow. She had no children to support her, and her husband's relatives abandoned her by the side of the road to die. The disciples took her in, fed her, restored her to good health, and found her a place to live. She heard the gospel and is now following Christ, going out in pairs to share it with others.

2. Sharing the Gospel

Many Hindus are willing to pray an immediate prayer of commitment, but they would be adding Christ to their pantheon of gods rather than submitting to him as the only Savior and Lord.

To address this challenge, the goal of follow-up visits is to start reading the *Ek Rasta* stories, giving them an understanding of the whole biblical narrative from Creation to Christ. The actual call to repent and believe is reserved until the end of the thirty-five studies.

The workers are careful to avoid attacking the household's existing faith. Instead, they allow the Scripture to reshape their worldview. As they read the story of Creation, they discover there is one true God who made heaven and earth. While studying the Ten Commandments, they realize God will judge those who worship idols. As they learn about Jesus' life, death, and resurrection, they come to understand God's plan of salvation.

By the end of the studies, they are ready to hear the call to repent, believe, and be baptized. Remarkably, 40 percent of households that start the *Ek Rasta* studies complete them, resulting in genuine conversion and becoming disciples of Jesus.

3. Training Disciples

The discipleship model is relational; the workers don't simply drop off an SD card and leave. Instead, they consistently return to guide the family through the thirty-five studies and the subsequent nine discipleship lessons. Households often complete multiple studies each week, and the workers return regularly to debrief the insights gained and lead the next study. While the household is working through the lessons, they are encouraged to share what they are learning with friends, neighbors, and relatives.

The training culminates when the trainees, having worked through the thirty-five studies, are ready to repent, believe, and be baptized. Baptism is presented as a commissioning to make disciples, mirroring the start of Jesus' ministry. They are taught to replicate what others did for them: knock on a door, visit a friend, share their story, and pray for needs, checking if the household is ready to start the same lessons they just finished.

A staggering 79 percent of disciples in the movement are visiting households near and far, sharing their story, healing the sick, and opening the Scriptures.

I talked to several disciples who were traveling into six, ten, and twenty villages. In each village, they had started multiple new churches. As we drove into some of these villages, waving to people along the way, Ravi would point and say, "We have a church in that house. We have a Bible study just beginning in that one."

4. Forming Churches

Church formation is a natural result of focusing on households for evangelism and discipleship. Because the groups have gathered around the Scriptures, prayed for one another, worshipped God, and learned to love one another through the initial studies, they begin to function as a body of believers. Church formation and discipleship are two ways of seeing the one reality. New disciples aren't just added to Christ; they're added to his people. There is no discipleship without church formation, and no church formation without discipleship.

In the transition from a group to a church, the new disciples read Acts 2:36–47 and identify the activities of a healthy church—repentance and faith, baptism, the Word, worship, fellowship around meals and the Lord's Supper, love and generosity, prayer, evangelism, and godly leadership.

Because these core activities are already embedded in the *Ek Rasta* studies, the new church members discover that there's nothing on that list that they need to start doing; they are simply identifying and formalizing their current practice.

5. *Multiplying Leaders*

I've never seen such a high percentage (79 percent) of volunteers involved in making disciples. Even those who aren't actively starting new households are helping to care for the families of those on the front lines.

I visited an extended family of farmers, including grandparents and the families of three brothers. The brothers decided that one of them would go to a distant location where there were no disciples or churches. He left his family for three months. During the day, he worked as a farmer; at night, he shared the gospel, made disciples, and planted churches. Meanwhile, the families back home supported his wife and children. No one told them to do this; there was no external funding—just a determination to follow Christ's call to take the gospel to every people and place. From this work, twenty-three household churches have emerged.

"This Cannot Be Happening!"

This unprecedented growth inevitably raised questions. Back at mission headquarters, the 2020 field report was causing a stir: The numbers from India were too good, reporting more new disciples and churches in this one field than in the rest of the world combined.

Questions were asked: *Are the figures inflated? Are the disciples genuine? Are the churches healthy?*

The situation mirrored the early church. In Acts, when thousands believed through Philip's work in Samaria, the leadership in Jerusalem sent Peter and John to investigate (Acts 8:5–14). When both Jews and pagan Gentiles turned to the Lord in Antioch, Jerusalem then sent Barnabas to investigate (Acts 11:19–22). In both cases, the reports were accurate, and despite the rapid growth, the work was solid.

The agency responded similarly, assembling a team of fourteen leaders from other fields in India. They gathered in early 2022 to investigate and assess the work. The team conducted interviews in four languages every day for three weeks, collecting data and compiling statistical reports.

The research showed that the various streams of disciples and churches were blessed with both depth and breadth. They found:

- 84 percent of the disciples could clearly explain the gospel.
- A high percentage understood the meaning of church, the Lord's Supper, and baptism.[3]
- 99 percent of disciples read or listened to the Scriptures at least weekly (and 70 percent read or listened to them daily).
- 79 percent of the disciples were actively sharing the gospel and making disciples. (One woman had led over two hundred people to Christ.)
- 99 percent of the churches planted in 2020 were still active in 2022. That means the disciples identified as a church, had local elders, practiced baptism and the Lord's Supper, studied the Scriptures together, gave regularly, and worshipped together.

Around 95,000 churches have been started, and there are hundreds of thousands of disciples making disciples. Despite this massive scale, the statistics show that quality has not been compromised. "People say we're going so fast that we don't care about the quality and depth of discipleship," says Gary. "But discipleship is a slow process every time. When pursued slowly and carefully, it results in rapid growth."

Ravi agrees: "Our most mature believers are no more than eight years in the Lord, but in that time, they've worked through the Bible six or seven times. They are continually taking new households through the *Ek Rasta* studies; they know the whole span of Scripture; they've studied doctrine and leadership development."

"The combination of the Holy Spirit and God's Word is the secret sauce that makes it all work," Gary adds. "The disciples meet often. They gather for worship and prayer, or all the men will get together. They'll meet for accountability and planning in making disciples and opening up unreached fields."

Anyone for Chai?

During my trip with Gary and Ravi, we would often stop for chai. At one stop, we were finishing our chai when Ravi asked for a few more minutes. He went over to the owner and said, "I'm a follower of *Yeeshu Maseeh* (Jesus Christ). We pray for people and teach the Bible. Can I share my story with you?"

He told them his story and prayed for the owner's family. Ravi asked Raj, the owner, about his family, his village—everything and everyone. By the time they finished talking, five men and boys were listening in.

Raj wanted to know more, so Ravi gave him an SD card to load on his phone. Ravi told him, "Watch the film with your family, listen to some of the lessons, then I'll give you a call, and we'll talk."

The entire interaction lasted less than thirty minutes. He wasn't after a quick conversion. He was looking for an open door into a whole community. Next time he's on the road, Ravi will visit Raj's village and meet his family.

As I watched their interactions, I thought of how God rescued Ravi as a teenager from the darkness of Hinduism and the pain of domestic violence. Over a cup of chai, he was ready and willing to share his story and invite Raj to learn more. Yes, he is a leader, but he's also the leader of thousands of ordinary people who do this every day. He's a leader who embodies this movement's identity.

I also thought about Gary, the seminary-trained Westerner, who came to South Asia twenty years ago in search of an insider like Ravi. He prayed, "Lord, can't you trust me with more than just this one guy?" But one was more than enough. God used that one guy to lead a movement of disciples, leaders, and churches.

In a movement, leaders are not known for their ministry, their preaching, or their administrative abilities; they are known for the disciples, workers, and pioneers they launch.

That's what it takes to see a movement of God that will sweep through regions of the world numbering in the billions. This movement will change the lives of people like Raj, the chai shop owner, and his family.

Transformed lives are at the heart of every movement of God. The Word is spreading in the power of the Spirit through God's people, freeing the captives.

You may not yet be seeing a multiplying movement, but you can listen for the stories of changed lives. That's how a movement begins.

Reflect and Act

While the story of Ravi, Gary, and the movement in India is unique, its lessons are universal. This isn't just a regional story about a seminary-trained outsider and a formerly outcast insider, or even just about Raj, the chai shop owner, and his community; it's a story about God and how he works in the world. To apply these lessons, this section challenges you to reflect on the movement dynamics presented in the story and to live them out in your own context.

As you reflect, remember the three essentials of a multiplying movement:

A movement's *Identity* mirrors the life and ministry of Jesus: obedient to the Word, dependent on the Holy Spirit, and faithful to the mission.

A movement's *Strategy* provides a clear path for expressing *Identity* in action—entering, gospeling, discipling, forming churches, and multiplying leaders.

A movement's *Methods* serve its *Strategy* and must be simple, effective, and contagious.

Movement Dynamics

Movements allow vision and action to fuel learning. Gary and Ravi's God-sized vision to reach India drove their learning in the field. Their *Identity* motivated them to act. Implementing their *Strategy* led to effective *Methods,* such as the *Ek Rasta* studies.

Movements have a clear pathway from engagement to multiplication. The movement's *Strategy* began with sharing the gospel with people far from God and led to multiplying disciples, churches, and leaders. There are no gaps. Every disciple understands the *Strategy* and is trained to execute it.

Movements use effective* Methods *to amplify impact. The right *Methods* amplify the movement's influence. The messengers carry inexpensive microSD cards. If the messengers can't read, everyone can still listen to the Bible stories and study together in their local language.

Movements go slow to go fast. The process moves slowly at first. The call to repent, believe, and be baptized comes only *after* the thirty-five studies are completed.

Usually, the workers journey with a family for six months until they are firmly rooted in their faith. After baptism, new disciples are trained and sent out to reach other households, resulting in rapid and healthy growth.

Movements work with families and social networks, not just individuals. Not every member of the household may be ready to repent and be baptized, but all have been involved in the process, making it less likely for the gospel to divide families. The movement reaches whole family and social networks rather than isolated individuals, increasing the likelihood of church formation.

Movements work both near* and *far. To these disciples, "near" means their neighborhood or the next village, while "far" can mean villages hundreds of miles away—often involving long hours spent on buses.

Jesus' primary focus was Israel, but he also extended his ministry into the Gentile world. From the beginning, he cast a vision for Jerusalem, Judea, Samaria, and the ends of the earth—it's for every people and every place … *everywhere.* Movements always have an eye to the next field.

Applying the Pattern

Reflect

It should be clear that this movement is a work of God, a God who calls and energizes his people to go on a journey of discovery and faith. The journey may take years of hard work and learning. There are no shortcuts, but looking back, the progress is miraculous. God's Word is triumphing as it goes out in the power of the Spirit through some very ordinary people.

Act

Read Acts 13–14 and fill out the 4-Fields Discovery worksheet in appendix one.

- Identify how Paul and Barnabas model each of the activities also employed by Gary and Ravi.

    1. Enter unreached fields.
    2. Share the gospel.
    3. Train disciples.
    4. Form churches.
    5. Multiply leaders.

- How will you follow their example?

____

____

____

5

From the Skatepark to the World

California

Others, like seed sown on good soil, hear the word, accept it, and produce a crop—some thirty, some sixty, some a hundred times what was sown.

MARK 4:20

Troy and Rachel Cooper had a bold vision to multiply disciples and churches in one of America's most challenging cities. So, in 2018, they packed up their seven kids and, along with three other families, moved from Florida to Los Angeles.[1] Shortly after their arrival, they planted Movement Church right in their home.

Getting Started

In the early days of Movement Church, the team spent time meeting leaders and Christians, asking them, "What's your vision? What's God teaching you? What do you see him doing in your city, and what do you need?" The team searched for "Great Commission Christians"—those serious about Jesus' call to make disciples. They then trained these individuals in simple tools for gospel conversations and making disciples. If trainees applied their new knowledge, the team would offer coaching, helping them to troubleshoot using the 4-Fields strategy.[2]

In their determined search, the team tried different methods. Sometimes, this meant hopping in a car and driving two hours to meet someone for coffee, then turning around and heading home. Other times, they'd go out and share the gospel, looking for a person of peace. Despite their hard work, they initially saw very little fruit, baptizing only two or three people in the first couple of years.

In January 2020, the team devoted a month to prayer and fasting. Then COVID-19 hit.

During the pandemic, the team from Movement Church served at one of the outdoor events where hundreds of people gathered on Friday nights at locations scattered along the Orange County coast to worship God. For many, it became an opportunity to put their faith in Jesus and follow him in baptism.

Troy and his team were baptizing new believers when they met Shane Nassirian. Shane was a new believer who had come to the event with his two friends, who were ready for baptism.

After they baptized his two friends in the ocean, Troy and the team explained that baptism is the doorway to discipleship, telling them, "Jesus walked with his disciples, so we want to walk with you."

Their discipleship journey began that night over tacos. Leveraging the summer break, Troy and a team member, Rick Preato, stopped what they were doing to meet daily with the new disciples for the next two weeks. They trained them using simple tools for evangelism (411), discipleship (Commands of Christ), and a healthy church (Church Circle).[3]

Reflecting on those two weeks, Shane recalls: "I got close to

Troy and Rick, spent a lot of time hanging out. We'd go to cafés, and my friends would show up. We'd open the Word, go through the Commands of Christ, and three or four of my friends would be there. We collected people as we went."

Starting with Zeal

Troy and Rick spent time observing Shane in action. They watched him meet his friends, share his story, and cast a vision for discipleship and a church community modeled after Acts 2. Shane held a natural influence with his peers and seemed to know everyone. It became apparent that he was a person of peace—opening his whole network to the gospel message.

Soon after, Shane and his two friends hosted a night of worship at a local home, drawing thirty-six people. Shane shared the story of what God had done in his own life and asked if anyone was ready to follow Jesus. That night, they baptized four friends in the backyard pool. Troy and the team from Movement Church, who had prepared Shane for this moment of growth, watched the baptisms unfold.

The next day, Shane guided these new disciples through the same lessons he had used with Troy, interweaving discipleship and church formation from the outset.

The movement quickly spread among Shane's circle, including his friend DJ. One night, while celebrating a friend's birthday, DJ got drunk. Overwhelmed by despair, he started yelling, before running down to the beach in desperation. "I was the only sober one left," Shane recalls. "So I ran after him but lost him in the dark. Eventually, I found him lying face down in the water. I ran into the surf and pulled him out. He was weeping uncontrollably. I prayed for him and told him how much Jesus loves him."

The next morning, DJ announced, "I'm done with this life. I'm going to follow Jesus." Shane started walking with him in discipleship, just as Rick and Troy had done with him.

Despite the fruit, Shane resisted the idea of planting a church, especially if he had to lead it. However, his mind began to change when the group he was leading reached Lesson 10 in the Commands of Christ: Gather, which clarifies what a church truly is. Seeing all the people who were coming to Christ, he realized he needed to plant a church: "I felt God gave us a name for the church—Zeal."

When other Christians questioned the legitimacy of Zeal Church, Shane looked to the church in Jerusalem to ensure their new church was committed to the same pattern.

Shane admits the challenge of establishing local leadership: "We still hadn't appointed elders. We didn't want to do that just to appease our critics. We didn't want to artificially bring in people from outside simply because they were older. As we studied the Word, we realized how important it was that those shepherding were raised from within the body." Zeal Church prioritized spiritual maturity for their leaders, believing they should be "doing what a shepherd does" before they were officially appointed.

After twelve months, Zeal Church had grown to thirty or forty people and had planted its first church at Vanguard University. What began with an ocean baptism and tacos in Orange County was now expanding. Most members were young adults from the overlapping social networks of Shane and his friends. Some had turned away from drugs; others renounced the New Age and witchcraft, burning their idols and books on magic in a fire pit.

Zeal Church is just one example of Movement Church's fruit. Tracing its origins to the foundational work of Troy and Rachel Cooper and their initial Movement Church team, the network has grown to thirty-four church starts, ranging in size from six to fifty people. Three of these have achieved four generations of new churches. This expansive network is now making a national and global impact by deploying and supporting around thirty frontline workers who are making disciples and planting churches in the Middle East, Africa, Europe, and Asia.

Hey Man, Nice Shirt!

Troy was at the skate park with his kids when he spotted Max Doty, a nineteen-year-old hippie pro-skater wearing a T-shirt with Scripture on it. It said, "It's no longer I who live, but Christ lives in me." Troy called out, "Hey man, nice shirt!"

Thinking Troy was making fun of him, Max sat with him and started sharing the gospel.

As they talked, it became clear that Max had been praying for God to lead him to a community where he could learn how to plant churches. Meeting Troy was the answer to that prayer. Max shared his dilemma: "I moved here from Phoenix and have been a believer for just under a year. I've led eleven people to faith in Jesus. But I don't know what to do with them!" Without hesitation, Troy replied, "Then let's walk together."

Having grown up completely outside the church, Max knew nothing about discipleship. Although his mom grew up Catholic and his dad was Southern Baptist, neither was interested in God. Skate culture filled that vacuum and became Max's world. He picked up a skateboard when he was four and never looked back, excelling at the sport. When he was fifteen, Max smoked his first joint and immediately wanted more. Eventually, he was stealing money from friends and family to buy weed. He started sleeping around and got hooked on porn. As an angry atheist, his soundtrack was punk and hardcore.

Max played guitar and sang in a heavy metal band alongside a drummer named Atticus. Hoping to improve his performance, Max often got high. It was during these times that Atticus would talk to him about Jesus. Max remembers, "I'd be sitting there, stoned, and Atticus would be telling me about Jesus. He talked about the book of Revelation. He'd tell me, 'We're in the last days.' I was intrigued."

Then, in 2021, as Atticus was sharing about Jesus' return, God opened Max's heart, and the message broke through. "I felt a hand pressed on my chest," Max says. "I felt fear, but it was a selfless fear. I thought, *When Jesus returns, what's going to happen to the people I love?* I went home and prayed to Jesus with desperation. Jesus set me free."

Max began to recognize the idols in his life: "I opened the Bible, and God showed me that skateboarding, sex, and drugs were my gods." He felt a weight lift and knew that his life's purpose was to minister the love God had given to him.

Back to the Skatepark

When Troy first met Max at the skatepark, churches in the network were gathering almost every night across Southern California. As part of Max's training, Troy began taking him to a different church each evening. There, Max learned a simple method of discipleship called the 3-Thirds, and observed new disciples share the gospel and engage with the Word among people far from God.[4]

The following week, Max met some guys in Oceanside and led them to Christ. Troy's teenage sons, Malachi and Isaiah, chimed in with the next step: "You've gotta follow them up. You've gotta walk with them." They then trained Max to disciple the new converts using the 3-Thirds.

"When I saw Troy and his family, and the team doing the work, something clicked," Max says. "I felt that this is the kind of life I want to live. They taught me the skills. I knew how to win people to Christ, but I didn't know how to disciple them. I wanted to plant churches, but I thought I had to go to college and get educated first. Troy showed me from the Scriptures that you don't need to have a theology degree to plant a church."

This practical training finally showed Max how to fulfill his vision. "I've always wanted to gather my skater friends who came to know Jesus in a place where we could worship God, read his Word, eat together, and fellowship as believers. Troy showed me how to make that happen."

Return to Phoenix

Max wanted to stay in Southern California—the weather was great, the skating was good, he was close to the beach, and he'd never seen so much fruit in making disciples. However, after a month of walking every day with Troy and the team, God called him back to Phoenix. Max needed to go home and do what he'd seen done in Southern California.

The day after Max moved back to Arizona, his twin sister turned to Christ. She saw the change in him and called out to Jesus to set her free. Previously anxious and introverted, she soon began talking to everyone about what God had done in her life.

Max reached out to the people he had already led to Christ and planted a church in his parents' living room with just five people, including his sister and his friend Wyatt, along with a girl named Sydnie, whom he had led to Christ (and whom he would eventually marry).

Applying everything he learned in California, Max began training these new disciples in the basics—the 411 training, 3-Thirds discipleship, the Commands of Christ, and the Church Circle.[5] The church grew to sixty people, and within a year, some of them were leading their own churches.

Max says, "God was working among people who were LGBTQ+. We had a girl who was transgender. She was cutting herself and was suicidal. She came to faith in Jesus in tears and handed over the razor that she used to cut herself. God was moving among skaters and college students. We were baptizing people in my parents' pool every week."

But the fruit created a new challenge: Sixty young adults invading the home every week became overwhelming for Max's unbelieving parents. "God used that to disperse us," Max reflects. "We were sixty people in a home—who could reproduce that?"

Max challenged people to start their own churches, knowing they had already experienced the simple, reproducible form of church in his home. "After a year, we had leaders who were ready for the challenge," he says. "God was moving us from addition to multiplication." The one church became many, in Phoenix and across the country, as Max—while competing in skating events—shared the gospel and trained disciples wherever he went.

Back home, Max was praying one day when he received a clear vision: He saw himself sitting at the table with his parents, sharing the gospel with them. A week later, sitting at that same table, he shared the 3-Circles gospel outline with them and asked his parents, "Is anything stopping you from turning to Jesus?"[6] His mom responded, "It's like I've been waiting my entire life to hear this. We need this." His dad immediately agreed.

The family, who had previously smoked weed together, was now reading the Bible and praying together. What God started in Southern California was now growing in Phoenix.[7]

Troy maintained his connection with Max through regular calls and visits, watching him grow in his calling, character, and competency. Max was no longer a lonely man on the frontier, wondering what to do next; he was thriving as an active part of a worldwide community of practitioners.

Seeing the World Through Movement Eyes

Typically, we don't view new believers as disciple makers and church planters. Even if we do, we don't know how to train them in simple methods.

Troy says a movement of God requires three elements:

- *A big vision*: Many church leaders have a vision for a big church. However, God has a vision for cities and nations. Troy helped Shane see that only a movement of disciples and churches could reach Orange County.
- *A clear path*: Troy uses a simple 4-Fields strategy (Entry, Gospel, Disciples, Churches, Leaders).[8] The 4-Fields offers people like Shane a starting point and a clear direction to follow.
- *Simple tools*: When it comes to making disciples, most believers don't know what to do on Monday morning. No one has trained them. Troy modeled and trained Shane in simple, biblical methods such as the 411, the Commands of Christ, and the Church Circle. As Shane's friends came to Christ, he trained them and helped turn them into a community of disciples who make disciples.

A movement mindset is a different way of seeing the world. When Jesus called the first disciples, he didn't require years of training; he called them to follow him and promised to teach them how to fish for people. Then off they went. His strategy was to give the Great Commission to every disciple.

If our strategy for making disciples is "Come, sit, enjoy the band and listen to the sermon," we'll never see a movement. The good news is we can change that now by changing how we make the next disciple. Right from the start, let's teach them to follow and fish.

Reflect and Act

While the journeys of Shane in Orange County and Max—the former atheist skater equipped by Troy and his teenage sons— are unique, the lessons they offer are universal. This story, rooted in Troy and Rachel Cooper's bold vision to multiply disciples in a challenging city, is a powerful demonstration of how God uses simple obedience and reproducible methods to unleash multiplication.

As you reflect, remember the three essentials of a multiplying movement:

A movement's *Identity* mirrors the life and ministry of Jesus: obedient to the Word, dependent on the Holy Spirit, and faithful to the mission.

A movement's *Strategy* provides a clear path for expressing *Identity* in action—entering, gospeling, discipling, forming churches, and multiplying leaders.

A movement's *Methods* serve its *Strategy* and must be simple, effective, and contagious.

Movement Dynamics

Movements look for people of peace. Troy wasn't at the skatepark by chance; he was there with his sons because he's a great dad and because it was a public place where they could meet people who needed Jesus. Troy was applying a *Strategy*: looking for God-prepared people. He noticed a skater with a Bible verse on his T-shirt and reached out, thinking, *Maybe we can train him.*

Movements train and launch. Troy multiplied leaders by viewing emerging leaders not as dependent on him but as disciple makers and movement catalysts. He built a strong bond with them and trained them in *Methods* that enable immediate replication. This training equipped them to share the gospel, form discipleship groups focused on obedience to Christ's commands, and models how a discipleship group can become a healthy church. He welcomed these pioneers into a global community of practitioners and peers.

Movements ordain everyone. Troy practiced the priesthood of every believer. Shane doubted he could plant a church, but Troy and Rick saw his potential and provided the challenge, training, and coaching he needed to do it. Likewise, Max was a gifted evangelist, but he didn't know how to make disciples; Troy's discipleship training and coaching equipped him for multiplication.

Movements develop local leaders. As Shane and the new church studied the Scriptures, they concluded that shepherds should emerge from within the church, identified as those who are already doing what is required.

In Acts, Paul's mission was never complete until there were local shepherds. Those leaders were not imposed from the outside but emerged from within, requiring return visits from Paul or a team member to identify and develop them (Acts 14:23).[9]

Applying the Pattern

Reflect

At any given time, there are people like Shane Nassirian and Max Doty, who find themselves at turning points in their lives, open to what God is doing. Typically, the goal is to reach them and enfold them into the body of Christ, where they can learn and mature. Troy had a different approach. He wasn't just looking for converts; he aimed for disciple makers who would become church planters. From the start, he taught Shane and Max to follow Jesus and immediately fish for others. That's how movements multiply.

Act

Read Mark 1:14–39 and fill out the 4-Fields Discovery worksheet in appendix one.

- How does Jesus model each of these activities?

    1. Enter unreached fields.
    2. Share the gospel.
    3. Train disciples.
    4. Form churches.
    5. Multiply leaders.

- How will you follow his example?

____

____

____

6

Follow the Fruit

Indonesia

The harvest is plentiful, but the workers are few. Ask the Lord of the harvest, therefore, to send out workers into his harvest field.

LUKE 10:2

In 1993, Trevor moved from the United States to Indonesia with a singular goal: to multiply disciples and churches among unreached Islamic people groups. He taught at an evangelical seminary where the students spent their weekdays in class and went out on weekends to make disciples. To graduate, each student had to plant at least one church with twenty-five baptized disciples.

Get Into the Field and Learn

Trevor became a mentor to the students as they faced the challenge of planting churches in a Muslim context. As he watched and learned from his students, he identified a gap: Traditional churches were seeing little progress among Indonesia's unreached people groups (UPGs). Determined to change this, Trevor launched a pilot project focused on a large UPG. He recruited students to join him, hiring them to conduct two-week cultural surveys of the UPG as he watched for the most effective workers.

He looked for the sunburned hands—evidence of students who spent the most time in the field, riding their motorcycles as they went from house to house and village to village. Trevor selected a team of students and sent them to find a strategic place in this challenging, unreached people group. When one of them objected, "But we don't know anything!" Trevor responded, "Then when you learn something, let me know!" Through these short-term research projects, he chose four students to work with him after graduation. Their job was to identify fruitful practices. At that time, "fruitful" meant gaining one or two new disciples from the people group. It took this team two years to establish the first believer group.

Once a year, the team paused its disciple-making work to conduct ethnographic research and cultural analysis. Their routine was highly structured: Each morning, they prepared research questions for the day, then went into the field collecting answers. Each evening, they debriefed on what they had learned. This systematic approach provided them with critical insights into how God was forming and reproducing new groups. By analyzing these results, Trevor identified which workers were most fruitful and why.

Follow the Fruit

This annual discipline marked the beginning of decades of action and reflection, leading to the development of fruitful practices for a growing movement. Trevor's team maintained an experimental culture, driven by prayer and research, to identify what truly produced results—learning to "follow the fruit" in the following ways.

Lead with Prayer

Trevor and his team found that offering prayer was an effective way to connect with people. They learned that Islamic leaders commonly used a ritual where they would write Quranic verses on paper, pray over them, burn them, and give the ashes to the person to drink. The team members recognized that praying the Bible over the sick created an opportunity for evangelism and discipleship, a pattern they observed aligning with engagement models found in the Gospels and Acts.[1] Realizing that Islam was oriented around ritual prayers, not teachings, they developed pattern prayers that incorporated biblical content. As they trained new believers to use these structured prayers, leading with prayer became a fruitful practice.

Dialogue and Discovery, Not Debate

Another fruitful approach was to engage in strategic dialogue. They found that asking Muslims in Islamic training centers, "Have you ever experienced God?" was highly effective. Culturally, this was a strange question to ask, which reliably elicited the answer, "No," followed by the curious inquiry, "How *do* I experience God?"

This approach resonated profoundly because when faced with illness, demonic oppression, or financial hardship, they felt they had nowhere to turn. They wanted an encounter with God in the everyday struggles of life, making this a far more effective starting point than a debate. Through this relational dialogue, many Muslims became convinced that Jesus is Lord, leading to an ongoing discipleship journey to unpack what that involved.

By 2006, in just eight years, they had formed fifty-two groups of four to five disciples, reaching approximately 250 disciples among unreached people groups, and their rate of multiplication was accelerating.

In 2008, the groups learned a simple method of asking seven questions to help seekers and new believers discuss and obey God's Word.[2]

The method went like this:

1. Check-In

- What are you rejoicing in recently?
- What have you been challenged by recently?

2. Scripture and Discussion

Read a Bible passage. Have each person retell the story in their own words. Then ask the following questions:

- What have you learned today about God from this passage?
- What have you learned today about Jesus from this passage?
- What have you learned today about people from this passage?
- What will you do this week because of what you learned?
- With whom will you share this week what you learned from this passage?

Groups, Not Individuals

The team's field research revealed a stark contrast between outreach focused on individuals versus ministry within existing social groups. Workers who spoke to individuals started faster but couldn't sustain their momentum. One worker, who was the first to reach three discipleship groups, believed that the most effective method was to disciple individuals, partly due to safety concerns. However, this individual-focused worker stalled at three groups, which then dropped back to just two. Those who focused on natural social groups initially saw slower progress, but after six months, their disciples began to reproduce.

"In the culture, if you talk to someone alone, it is likely to be about a forbidden or shameful topic," Trevor explains. Conversely, when the gospel was discussed in natural groupings—such as "friends that were eating boiled peanuts late at night while they strummed guitars and sang"—it was viewed as socially acceptable and easily repeatable by new disciples.

Based on this insight, the team adjusted its training. They began coaching disciples to talk about the gospel naturally within groups of friends or family. The workers spent time chatting and listening out for local topics of interest. They then shared relevant truths from Scripture, referring to God's character and purposefully guiding the conversation toward Christ and the cross as the ultimate solution for those issues. Trevor calls this "transformation dialogue."

Find the Right People

Their twelve-month program to equip workers had good trainers and participants, but none of the trainees produced fruitful movement catalysts. Arif, a local leader, told Trevor, "We need to shut this down; it's not fruitful. We don't exist to run training events but to find the right people."

Instead of months of training, Arif suggested a single day to identify people who acted, using the day as a filter. He piloted this approach with a church of four hundred focused on reaching Muslims, asking them to select the 10 percent of their members most likely to engage this community.

Forty people attended the one-day training and, of those, four immediately started sharing the gospel and making disciples. Arif had found the right people.

Over the following months, these four individuals reported their progress and received additional training and coaching.

Arif and others have applied this one-day filter training to twenty churches. Within four years, the number of Muslims reached in underground churches exceeded the original size of the sending church.

Third, Not First Generation

Trevor and his team learned to look beyond the first generation of disciples and groups to the third generation.[3] This focus has become one of their driving principles. "Our eyes must be on getting to the third generation. That must drive us," Trevor explains. "I was once a roofer, and on the first day, the boss told me, 'There's only one thing you need to know—water flows downhill. When you're up there, think, if you were a raindrop and you fell, where would you slide?' In the same way, when we make disciples, we ask, 'Will this flow down to the third generation?' We apply that to everything we do."

This third-generation focus immediately exposed cultural and linguistic barriers. For example, in Indonesia, the Christian name for Jesus is *Yesus Kristus*. However, one of Trevor's researchers discovered that local Muslims widely misinterpret this name, believing *Yesus Kristus* was the result of sex between God and Mary, turning her into a goddess and Jesus into a half-man, half-god. Conversely, when the researcher asked about *Isa Al-Masih* (the Arabic name for Jesus Christ), these same Muslims held a far more biblical view, informed by the limited accounts of Jesus within the Quran and Islamic tradition.[4]

"We realized that using *Isa Al-Masih* instead of *Yesus Kristus* would make it easier to lead people to surrender to Jesus," Trevor says. "This approach allows the message to flow more naturally and helps form groups in the third generation. That's how we multiplied into thirty generations of disciples and groups."

This third-generation strategy also has implications for leadership, as illustrated by the experience of Amatt, a traditional church planter. His home church sent him to gather a congregation and plant a church, which he did, leading twenty-five people to Christ. Yet, Amatt quickly realized the burden: "All the weight was on my shoulders. I had to invest in all those people, and it was always on me. The congregation enjoyed what I gave them, but they didn't take on any responsibility. Why? That's what I'd modeled."

However, when Amatt adjusted his focus to reaching the third generation, his priority shifted from delivering everything to the congregation to investing in the disciples so they could carry the load. Now, he says, "The responsibility lies with all of us. That's the only way to reach the third generation and beyond."

Seize Opportunities

Indonesia is prone to natural disasters, including volcanic eruptions, tsunamis, floods, mudslides, and hurricanes. Through their commitment to action and reflection, the team learned to integrate disaster relief with disciple making.

In 2018, a small tsunami hit an island to the east of where the local team lived and worked. Trevor and his teammate, Reza, responded. "I was the construction guy, and Reza was there to make disciples," Trevor says.

They met a widow who had lost her home and asked her to list five to eight families who would commit to working alongside her on the construction and supporting one another. "'We want to help you build the foundation for your house,' we told her. 'But it has to start and finish this week because we have to go home.'"

The families agreed to help each other. Trevor worked with them and gave them funds for the steel and a concrete foundation. The community provided the labor, with every family sending at least one man to do the work—except the widow, who cooked for them all. By the end of the week, the rebar and forms were in place for each foundation, and the workers said they could pour the concrete themselves.

After researching how concrete blocks are made, Reza had an idea. He suggested the group start a concrete-block-making business. "We provided enough money for the first truckload of sand, cement, and forms," Trevor says. "We helped them figure out how many units they needed to make and sell to afford the next truckload." The concept resonated, and people shared the idea with their relatives and friends. Soon, seven separate businesses were up and running.

Reza and the team of local evangelists he trained visited these new businesses. The combination of practical help and sharing the gospel led many to turn to Christ, and they planted simple house churches. Today, thousands are following Christ on that island.

Develop Apostolic Agents

In the early days, Trevor consistently invested in local leaders, who became movement catalysts alongside him. They developed leaders from within the movement and also "adopted" pioneering leaders—those who had made a good start independently but lacked the necessary training, coaching, and a supportive "tribe."

They learned to identify and empower "Apostolic Agents"— individuals with initiative and passion to open new areas for the gospel. An agent's primary role is to strengthen new believer groups, establish and develop local leaders, connect them to the broader movement, and then move on to a new, unreached area. Trevor discovered that mentoring these agents in high-impact practices was key to significantly increasing the fruitfulness of their teams.

Arif is a powerful example of an Apostolic Agent at work. Raised in a Muslim family, Arif surrendered to Christ and was baptized at eighteen. Aged twenty, he enrolled in seminary. To graduate, he was required to plant a church, which he accomplished in 1993.

In 2004, Arif experienced his second assignment. God called him away from his role as a pastor to become an evangelist and a pioneer among Muslims: "The Spirit convicted me that the Great Commission was not to gather as many people as you can but to go to the nations and make true disciples of Jesus." With a wife, four children, and no salary, he finished his role at the church and laid down his identity as a pastor.

Arif and his wife fasted and prayed for forty days with a map of Indonesia spread out before them. As they prayed, God gave them a verse from the book of Acts: "You will receive power when the Holy Spirit comes on you; and you will be my witnesses in Jerusalem, and in all Judea and Samaria, and to the ends of the earth" (Acts 1:8). On the thirty-ninth day of their fast, God showed Arif a picture of a man he knew but hadn't heard from in two years: Joyo.

When he called Joyo, Arif recalls, "His voice was trembling. He told me he was standing by the railway tracks, intending to step in front of a train."

Joyo was desperate: "I've tried following Jesus," he told Arif, "but I was thrown out of my village, separated from my wife and children. They destroyed my home. I can't go on."

Arif replied, "Jesus *is* helping you. That's why I'm calling!"

Joyo stepped back from the tracks, and the next day, Arif drove eighteen hours to find him. Joyo became Arif's first disciple.

Over the next few months, Arif made the long journey to strengthen this disciple's faith. As Joyo grew, they rode from village to village on a motorcycle, sharing the gospel from morning to evening. Every night, they reflected, evaluated, planned for the next day, and prayed for the individuals they had met. Arif says, "God was teaching me to discover places and people, find those who were receptive, and understand local needs."

After three years without much discernible fruit, Arif lost hope. He stopped trying, changed his phone number, and cut all contact—telling no one, not even Joyo. As he waited on God, he felt, *I'm done. I can't go back to the field.* Ten months later, however, he decided to make the long journey back to find Joyo. Surely Joyo had given up by now.

To Arif's surprise, Joyo came to meet him with five new believers. "Remember when we visited such and such a place? This one is from that area. Remember this man who was healed? Remember how we were kicked out of that village? This guy is from there."

Arif wept, thinking, *God, this movement isn't about me. It's about you.* He realized that the years of hardship were the planting season, and what he was witnessing were the first fruits. Now, he knows his role is to equip people like Joyo. "There's only one of me," he concludes, "but thousands can own the Great Commission."

Today, Arif leads multiplying streams of disciples and churches, reaching beyond four generations.

Depth *and* Breadth

In 2008, Trevor attended his first training on disciple making movements, led by David Watson, a movement catalyst and author. Trevor was scheduled to present a case study. As he was preparing to leave Indonesia, his team kept handing him scraps of paper with the latest counts of new groups.

He had been trusting God for a lifetime goal of two hundred communities. When he added up the figures on the plane, the team had already reached about 450 disciples from a Muslim background, in 110 groups. The numbers astonished him. *Either I've set the goal too low*, Trevor thought, *or I'm going to die soon!*

At the event, God gave him a much greater vision: twenty thousand groups. From that point on, the existing communities began multiplying at a rate of 60 percent annually, a pace that continued for the next fifteen years. Simple, biblical, and reproducible methods facilitated the rapid growth.

At the heart of this movement are small groups of five to six disciples who read, obey, and pass on God's Word. This size is intentional: They're less likely to attract unwanted attention in majority Islamic areas. These communities function as churches linked in clusters of fifteen.

Trevor explains that the book of Acts uses the word "ecclesia" (church) in three ways: small gatherings in homes, the church across a city, and the church throughout a region.[5] He believes that each form of church is necessary for the movement to flourish and expand. But such fruitfulness carries a burden. Growth is never problem-free; it always brings challenges, such as moral failures, money issues, conflicts, or persecution. Trevor and Arif's teams try to handle these issues at the most basic level, involving senior leaders only in the most difficult and strategic matters. The movement remains strong by empowering people.

This empowerment allows the movement to embrace both growth and depth. "We often hear, 'We want quality, not quantity,'" Trevor says. "Show me the verse that says we don't want quantity.

The book of Acts reports both quantity and quality; they go hand in hand. I grew up on a farm, and I've never heard an apple grower say, 'I want quality, not quantity.' I've never heard a dairy farmer say, 'I want quality but not quantity.' No farmer says that. They all want both. Quality and quantity are connected symbiotically. They belong together. That's why we've made such good progress toward a multiplying movement of disciples and churches. Almost every quarter, when the counts come in, I weep about what God has been doing."

Reflect and Act

While the Indonesian context is unique, the principles are universal. This isn't just a story about success in a challenging region. It's a story of how God uses field-driven learning and the disciplined formation of leaders to establish a movement that depends on him for fruitful practices. To apply these lessons, this section challenges you to reflect on the movement dynamics presented in the story and to live them out in your own context.

As you reflect, remember the three essentials of a multiplying movement:

A movement's *Identity* mirrors the life and ministry of Jesus: obedient to the Word, dependent on the Holy Spirit, and faithful to the mission.

A movement's *Strategy* provides a clear path for expressing *Identity* in action—entering, gospeling, discipling, forming churches, and multiplying leaders.

A movement's *Methods* serve its *Strategy* and must be simple, effective, and contagious.

Movement Dynamics

Movements allow vision and action to drive innovation. Trevor is a rare blend of professor and practitioner, and the leaders of the movement share that ethos. The driving force behind learning is an unwavering vision for disciples and churches in every people group and among the majority population. That reflects their *Identity* as a movement. The result is innovation, not for its own sake, but in pursuit of their *Strategy* for multiplying disciples and churches. The gap between the actual and the ideal motivates and renews this movement as they implement their *Strategy* and test their *Methods*.

Movements identify fruitful practices. These practices support the movement's growth in both depth and breadth. A good farmer plans and works for both quality *and* quantity. Both are biblical priorities. These practices include transformational dialogue in evangelism, focusing on groups rather than individuals, Discovery Bible Study for discipleship, and simple *Methods* for church formation and leadership development. When starting the first group of disciples, the workers learn to ask, "What will it take to reach the third generation?" They recognize pioneers by observing who implements the training.

Movements widen the circle of leadership. Trevor serves as the movement's founder, but he hasn't done it alone. Early on, he identified the Indonesians God called to serve with him as part of a founding group. Arif is one of those leaders. This is a movement of movement catalysts. Despite its size, only twenty-two movement catalysts are receiving financial support. Most workers are volunteers.

Movements have multiple streams of workers. The network has successfully attracted movement pioneers who previously worked independently. Many of them were frustrated because their evangelism efforts hadn't resulted in multiplying disciples and churches. They joined the movement for training, coaching, and peer support.

Movements embrace God's discipline. Arif exemplifies many leaders in this movement whose *Identity* is shaped by God. Having left security and success to focus on making disciples, he experienced deep discouragement and lost hope, but the Lord rescued him. As the movement grows, God calls, tests, and molds leaders like Arif as they learn fruitful practices. The Lord shapes the hearts of those he uses; there are no shortcuts. He taught both Arif and Joyo profound lessons that would prepare them for what lay ahead. These wilderness years are not wasted. Arif's story reminds us that God forms movement leaders both in character and effectiveness. Sometimes, it takes years for breakthroughs to happen.

Movements outgrow the founder/s. God calls founding leaders who embody the original vision and discover fruitful practices. Paradoxically, to grow, the founder or founding group must let go of control and empower the movement to own its *Identity*, *Strategy*, and *Methods*, no longer dependent on the founder. The movement becomes a cause rather than an institution. Trevor is a founder who has enabled this movement to extend beyond his direct leadership and control. The bond that holds the movement together is a shared commitment to a common cause and to each other.

Applying the Pattern

Reflect

In a movement, learning and doing are always integrated; the field is the classroom. When Jesus called his first disciples, he didn't enroll them in a lecture hall. Instead, he told them to follow him and promised to teach them how to fish for others. Their growth in knowing him and their growth in making disciples were one and the same process. They learned by following.

Similarly, when Jesus sent out the Seventy-Two ahead of him to carry out the mission, they returned with joy, saying, "Lord, even the demons submit to us in your name" (Luke 10:17). It was only by *doing* the work that they gained this deeper knowledge of Christ's authority and power. These lessons could not be imparted to passive listeners in a classroom. In a movement, learning and doing are interwoven. This is what drove Trevor. His Great Commission vision led him to action, and his action drove the learning.

Act

Review the pattern of 3-Thirds discipleship.[6] Find at least one other person and practice 3-Thirds discipleship. Do the first Command: Repent and Believe.

____

____

____

____

7

High Stakes, Deep Faith

Ghana

Very truly I tell you, unless a kernel of wheat falls to the ground and dies, it remains only a single seed. But if it dies, it produces many seeds.

JOHN 12:24

Isaac Aziz grew up in a Muslim family in northern Ghana. In his community, converting to Christianity was seen as betrayal. So when Isaac turned to Christ, the consequences were immediate—his family disowned him, and his own father authorized his killing. But God was at work: Following two failed attempts on his life, one of his attackers turned and believed.

Amid this dangerous reality, God spoke to Isaac through the words of the prophet Isaiah: "I will also make you a light for the Gentiles" (Isaiah 49:6). Commissioned by this word, Isaac began openly sharing Jesus with Muslims and regularly leading evangelistic teams.

Isaac's conviction to fulfill this call was unwavering. When a local church offered him a paid position as a pastor, he declined, explaining that his passion was to go out "beyond the four walls of the church." Similarly, he turned down an invitation to start a church in Accra, Ghana's vibrant capital, because it's where most of the Christians live—as Isaac says, "It's choked with churches."

Instead of accepting a comfortable ministry role, Isaac left his secure government job and moved back to the Muslim-majority north. Though his relatives didn't welcome him, Isaac found favor with the village chief—an old friend who gave him some vacant land. With help from some disciples, he and his wife built a mud-brick house, and God provided the money for a tin roof.

Meanwhile, thousands of miles away in New Albany, Indiana, Terry and Amy Ruff were serving as mission pastors in their local church. Hoping to mobilize workers for global missions, they led a Perspectives course.[1] Instead, it shook *their* world, and they caught a vision for church planting movements. The next missionaries the church sent out were Terry and Amy.

Their destination was northern Ghana, West Africa, where they were tasked with training locals to plant churches among the majority Muslim population. They arrived in Accra in 2009. While preparing for the twelve-hour journey north to their new home, they met Isaac. Realizing that they shared an interest in orality—the practice of using stories to convey biblical truth—they agreed to form a partnership. In Ghanaian villages, 80 percent of the people are oral learners, so they began using Bible storying to share the gospel, which proved effective. The team strategically invested in building a studio to produce audio Bibles and resources in local languages. Since every family has a cell phone, they made the audio available on microSD cards, which cost $5 to produce. Many people wept when they received their first copy of the Scriptures. As things grew, they provided tablets to leaders so they could burn and hand out the microSD cards themselves.

They implemented best practices for multiplying movements,

adapted their approach for an oral audience, and introduced 3-Thirds discipleship groups.[2] As a result, the number of new disciples, baptisms, and groups increased. However, despite successfully planting over thirty churches, their progress was still marked by addition, not multiplication. This stark realization catalyzed a paradigm shift.

Clear Strategy, Simple Methods

In 2015, Isaac and the Ruffs traveled to Burkina Faso for training with Curtis Sergeant, a movement catalyst. The trip proved to be a turning point. By the end of the two-week training, Isaac had already started two churches in the country and handed them over to local workers! Having caught the vision, Isaac set a goal of one church for every ten households in northern Ghana. According to Terry, "He's been going crazy ever since!"

Curtis's training simplified their entire approach, making every method easily reproducible. They streamlined the 3-Thirds discipleship process and focused on building a ministry "tool pouch." Curtis encouraged them to fill the pouch with simple tools and trust the Holy Spirit to guide them in using the right tools at the right time. The new kit included the 3-Circles for sharing the gospel and the Any-3 method (anyone, anywhere, anytime), tailored for sharing Christ with Muslims.[3]

But methods alone weren't enough. "The tools are great, but unless we use MAWL (Model, Assist, Watch, Launch) with new workers, nothing will happen," Terry emphasizes. Experienced workers *Model* the tool, then *Assist* new workers as they try it, *Watch* them use it independently, and finally *Launch* them into full ministry. "They need to see that the tools work, then try them out themselves, and finally receive feedback and help. Then it clicks," Terry explains. "Otherwise, it's just another class, and they never implement it."

This hands-on, modeling approach was key to overcoming barriers to sharing the gospel. Knowing some disciples weren't sharing because they struggled with illiteracy or didn't know what to say, the trainers modeled a simple Creation-to-Christ story and had the disciples memorize it.[4] Once the disciples saw it modeled and practiced it themselves, they gained the confidence and content to share. They trained disciples to identify one hundred people in their network who were far from God, select the five most receptive individuals, and pray daily for their sphere of influence. They also identified the next five people to connect with. At each gathering, disciples waited on God, allowing him to direct them to individuals or places. By teaching these simple methods, the team enabled every disciple to become a disciple maker. Some even became "superspreaders" of the gospel.

Terry emphasizes the importance of empowering every disciple: "When the disciples learn they can baptize people, that they can lead others to Christ and facilitate a discipleship group— they go for it!" he explains. "The heart of a movement is that everyone knows how simple and important it is for them to be a disciple maker. They have the skills, motivation, and authority to do what Jesus commanded."

Finding People of Peace

Isaac trained workers to enter unreached villages and offer to pray for people. He taught the disciples to use a simple BLESS model when offering prayer.

- **B**ody health
- **L**abor of your hands

- Economic life
- Social relations
- Spiritual identity

Terry explains how this simple prayer identifies receptive people. "If they are a person of peace, they invite you to their home to pray for their family and neighbors. When you return a second time, they invite others to hear more stories about Jesus. Once they understand what it means to be a disciple, the group is often baptized at the same time. Then they start to discover what a church is. It happens naturally."

This approach has led to dramatic, life-altering results. Once, Isaac traveled to Niger, where he and a local worker he was training spent two days fasting and praying before setting out, intent on finding a house of peace. They fueled up and drove out of town to a remote area.

Their journey led them to a well, where they stopped to greet the women drawing water and ask about their village. Isaac entered the first house that welcomed them and prayed the BLESS prayer. An elderly woman asked them to pray that her son, missing for eighteen years, would return home. They prayed, shared the gospel, and left with an invitation to return.

Their faithful prayers were answered: A year later, the long-lost son finally returned home. Today, that village has a vibrant church, led by his son. The grandson, born soon after the son's disappearance, is now eighteen and leads the ministry established in the village.

Focus on a Few Who Multiply

Curtis taught Isaac that to reach the many, he must focus on the few who are multiplying. Isaac implemented that strategy, leading to rapid, sustainable growth. In 2017, there were 1,650 baptisms and 380 new groups. In 2018, there were 3,511 baptisms—including people from forty-six different tribes—and 797 new groups. They were no longer just adding one church at a time. They were planting generations of new disciples and healthy, multiplying churches.

Four years later, in 2019, over three thousand people were involved in discipleship groups and churches. By 2022, that number had grown to 4,700 groups, with an average of six adults each—nearly 25,000 adult disciples.

What began in northern Ghana has spread to other West African countries. Isaac and other disciples have sparked movements in Sierra Leone, Burkina Faso, Nigeria, Guinea, Togo, and Benin. They define a movement as comprising at least one thousand disciples across one hundred groups or churches, with four streams spanning four generations of churches. One of those streams has multiplied to twenty-nine generations.

To sustain this rapid, wide-reaching growth, they established four levels of leadership, ranging from regional segments to the local village level.

- Segment leaders
- Section leaders
- Subsection leaders
- Village leaders

Every leader functions as both a coach and a person being coached. Because segments are too large to cover on foot, these leaders are given a motorcycle. The other leaders live within walking distance of the leaders they coach.

Movements and Money

Terry and Amy emphasize that ministry must be driven by calling, not financial compensation: "We've learned the hard way that this is a calling, and you don't want people doing it just for a paycheck. Many people will come out of the woodwork if you pay them. Eventually, you find they aren't true disciples; meanwhile, you've wasted a lot of energy and money. We use money as sparingly as possible, first because we don't have much; and second, because it's better for the movement not to rely on outside funding."

All the churches are self-sustaining and committed to meeting local needs. Typically, churches give two to three dollars each week, using the funds to send church members to unreached villages and assist struggling families.

"We don't support workers based on potential," Terry says. "We help someone because they are already doing what God has called them to do and plan to expand. We pay our movement catalysts, but only *after* they have pioneered a movement and shown their commitment."

In the early days, they attempted to launch several businesses—including a tree farm, a cell phone charging service, grinding mills, and a taxi service—hoping they would fund the ministry, but the ventures failed, costing energy and money. "Our movement catalysts want to make disciples, not run businesses," they explain.

Their leaders rely on simple, indigenous means of survival, such as vegetable gardens, fishing, and raising chickens, rabbits, and bees. "They survive on very little. That's what movements do. Everyone is paying a price."

Despite keeping costs low, they face growth challenges: "As the movement expands, we need more motorcycles to keep pace."

They currently have twelve bikes but recognize that they will soon need more. The ultimate question, Terry says, remains: "What will happen when we're no longer present and outside funding runs out?"

"We need to find a sustainable way to fund growth," they conclude. "Movements thrive when resources come from the harvest itself, as indigenous leaders and churches develop their own solutions. A movement's strength depends on its willingness to make sacrifices."

So Much Was at Stake!

After I finished my interview with Terry and Amy, I turned off the recording, and we chatted. I commented on the strength of their partnership, and they laughed wryly. "It hasn't always been that way!" they confessed. I asked if I could keep recording as they described the spiritual battles they fought in Ghana.

Their battles began on a profoundly personal level. Eight months after they arrived, Amy discovered a lump in her breast—it was cancer. She was forced to spend nine months in the United States undergoing treatment. Terry supported her by flying in from Ghana each time she needed surgery. Amy is now in remission.

The couple has been robbed five times. Once, an intruder used a crowbar to remove two doors and held Amy at knife-point. They have faced family crises at home and the death of a teammate on the field.

Then came a tragic betrayal: Isaac began an adulterous relationship, claiming God had told him in a dream to take a second wife. When Terry challenged him, Isaac retaliated, announcing he would return to Islam and take his disciples with him. "Your dream doesn't trump the Word of God!" Terry warned him.

Months passed in painful silence without any sign of repentance. Then Isaac returned, broken. "I feel like a ram caught in the thicket deep in the bush, and I want to come back," he confessed. Terry and a local pastor spent the next eighteen months leading Isaac through a process of restoration before he returned to ministry.

But Satan struck again. Another key leader fell morally and refused correction when Isaac and Terry confronted him. When he finally broke, he wept for hours, but he secretly continued to live in sin. For several years, he maintained a façade, lying about the number of his groups and baptisms. When the truth came out, the leader was stepped down. A team of leaders revisited each of his areas, uncovering widespread deception. Although it was a painful discovery, in most places, they found a faithful remnant that continues to grow in maturity and fruit.

"What keeps you going?" I asked Terry.

"There was so much at stake!" he insisted. "We had to keep going."

Amy summarized the three things she's learned through these trials: "First, we promised to always walk through the doors that God opens. Second, God wants this more than we do. Third, this is not our home; this is not where we rest; this is not where everything is good. Heaven is where we will receive our reward. One day, we will find rest and enjoy his glory around the throne."

Reflect and Act

While the story of Isaac, Terry, and Amy is unique, its lessons are universal. This isn't just a powerful narrative of multiplication; it's a testament to God's relentless commitment to his church, despite betrayal, persecution, and deep personal cost. To apply these lessons, this section challenges you to reflect on the movement dynamics presented in the story and to live them out in your own context.

As you reflect, remember the three essentials of a multiplying movement:

A movement's *Identity* mirrors the life and ministry of Jesus: obedient to the Word, dependent on the Holy Spirit, and faithful to the mission.

A movement's *Strategy* provides a clear path for expressing *Identity* in action—entering, gospeling, discipling, forming churches, and multiplying leaders.

A movement's *Methods* serve its *Strategy* and must be simple, effective, and contagious.

Movement Dynamics

Movements are initiated by God. God used the Perspectives course to call Terry and Amy to Ghana. When they arrived, the Lord connected them with Isaac, their key national partner, with whom they served for fourteen years.

Movements require paradigm shifts. They had a *Strategy* that led to over thirty new churches, but they soon hit a wall. The breakthrough came when they incorporated best practices gleaned from other fields. God brought Curtis Sergeant into the picture to guide Isaac and the Ruffs through their necessary paradigm shift. They learned to simplify their *Methods*, using ones that were not only powerful but also easily reproducible.

Movements need local ownership. God used Terry and Amy as catalysts. But the movement was led by insiders. The shift began when Isaac embraced the vision and something changed in his *Identity*. After his training with Curtis, he returned home to equip and train national leaders. Terry and Amy stepped back from the frontline, transitioning their role to one of equipping, loving, and discipling Isaac and the national leaders.

Movements use money wisely. The Ruffs redefined their use of outside funds, dedicating resources only to fund multiplication, not addition. The churches are taking responsibility to give from their own poverty to spread the movement and care for the needy.

Movements hold an eternal perspective. God shapes *Identity* through adversity. From the first year, the Enemy attacked Amy's health. The battle continued with illnesses, break-ins, and family crises. Two senior leaders committed adultery; one never truly repented. The Ruffs stood firm throughout these attacks, understanding the high stakes. They walked obediently through the doors God opened and trusted him to work through their weakness. Their hope was in their heavenly reward, not in what this world can offer. Satan opposes the spread of the Word. He is defeated, but the battle rages as we lead people from the dominion of Satan to God. Though messengers suffer, they remain in God's care.

Applying the Pattern

Reflect

Jesus' *Identity* was forged through his baptism and wilderness testing, and ours will be forged in battle as we pursue movements of disciples and churches.

Jesus modeled surrender: He submitted to his Father's Word, depended on the Holy Spirit, and remained faithful to his mission. He won the victory before he stepped onto the public stage of history.

We don't rise above the Lord Jesus. If he experienced attacks, so will we. But we are not alone. God will use these battles to make us like Christ and advance his cause.

Act

Read Acts 27–28:14.

- How does God shape Paul as a movement pioneer?
- How has God been shaping your identity?
- How can you cooperate with his work in you?

8

We Are the *Talamiz Al-Masih*

Lebanon

See, I am doing a new thing! Now it springs up; do you not perceive it? I am making a way in the wilderness and streams in the wasteland.

ISAIAH 43:19

James and Hope live in Beirut, an Arab city familiar with bombs, riots, and war. They know the smell of burning tires, the sound of distant shelling, the sight of a city's skyline choked with smoke and dust. In 2020, a massive explosion flattened many of Beirut's buildings, killing two hundred people.[1]

After the atrocity, James and Hope began a daily routine: Every morning from 6 to 8 a.m., they walked through the rubble and prayed over the devastated neighborhoods. Using only their basic Arabic and offering nothing more than prayer, they began to forge connections with those they met. People welcomed them into the ruins. One morning, they met Leila sitting outside her damaged home, slowly sipping her coffee. The blast had left her with serious injuries.

When Leila asked them why they were there, James and Hope replied, "We're praying for the community in the name of Jesus and asking for God's blessing." She accepted their offer of prayer, and as they prayed, she wept, hoping she would somehow find a place to stay. Just a few days later, James and Hope returned to the neighborhood, only to discover an aid agency had selected Leila as the very first person in her community to have her home repaired. They finished the work in three days, leaving her home in a better state than before the explosion.

Leila exclaimed, "This is because of your prayers!" She trusted in Christ and became the first new disciple baptized by James and Hope. Soon, eight women were regularly gathering at Leila's newly repaired home to discuss stories about Jesus.

With a growing group of new believers, James and Hope realized they needed to move beyond their rudimentary Arabic. So, they met daily with a language teacher to learn stories about Jesus in the local dialect. Then they went to Leila's home to share the stories with the group and ask the questions they had memorized. Leila would then lead the discussion. This disciple-making process extended to Leila's family. She shared the gospel with her eighty-five-year-old grandmother, who told them, "Pray for my son to get a job. If God answers, I'll believe." The answer came swiftly: The next day, her son secured a job as a security guard. The grandmother turned and believed and was baptized.

Through these experiences, James and Hope learned how to reach unreached neighborhoods, how to get invited in for coffee, how to pray for needs and see God answer, how to launch Bible discovery groups and identify a leader—all this while they were still learning Arabic. Through these early breakthroughs, God was preparing them for an open door in another part of the country.

Talamiz Al-Masih

The new assignment brought them into contact with Ibrahim, a Muslim from a turbulent region controlled by rival clans engaged in crime. A drug dealer with thirty years' experience, Ibrahim had served a decade in jail for murder. It was there that he cried out to God. Once free and back home, God had awoken him one morning and told him to go and wait outside for a messenger.

Meanwhile, a German missionary was driving through that same dangerous region. His rental car company was tracking his movements and grew concerned that the vehicle had been stolen. Knowing the area was notorious, they remotely disabled the car, which rolled to a stop directly outside Ibrahim's house. Ibrahim was standing right there, waiting for the messenger God had promised.

Through a translator, the German shared the gospel. Ibrahim immediately believed and was baptized. The missionary soon returned to Germany, but before he left, he connected Ibrahim with James and Hope.

The couple met Ibrahim and his family of sixteen children. A family member said, "I wish you'd come earlier. Since meeting Jesus, he no longer gets drunk, he no longer beats us, and he's given up cocaine."

But not all family members felt the same. James accompanied Ibrahim to share the gospel with his sister's family. When Ibrahim's Islamist nephew came home and found out his parents wanted to follow Jesus, the young man exploded in rage. He threw a rock at his father, missing him but striking Ibrahim and sending him to the hospital. Ibrahim, who was renowned in the village and known by the epithet "*al-kafir al-awwil*" (our number one infidel), responded to the attack with forgiveness and love.

His astonishing reaction spread, and he became known instead as "*rajul almaghfira*" (the man of forgiveness).

James began training Ibrahim to make disciples. Within two weeks, two of Ibrahim's own relatives were ready for baptism. However, Ibrahim didn't know how to baptize them. James met with them, and while a bathtub filled with water, he guided them through a study on baptism. James baptized the first relative, showing Ibrahim how to baptize the next.

When his turn came, Ibrahim flatly refused. James gently but firmly insisted, and reluctantly, Ibrahim performed the second baptism. As he emerged from the bathroom, he stared at his wet hands in disbelief, exclaiming, "What did I just do?" The former drug dealer realized that God had made him for this.

Making disciples came at a high cost. After Ibrahim had gained his first few believers, Islamists arrived at his house under the cover of darkness and started shooting. His sons, who were not yet believers, ran for their guns and fought off the attackers. Despite the opposition, Ibrahim stood firm, declaring, "My life is a sacrifice for the Lord Jesus, and I will not turn away from following him."

As Ibrahim's faith grew, God was working within his family. His son Ali, who had been present when the German mission-ary's car broke down, soon started his own spiritual journey. Ali knew nothing about Jesus, but the events he had witnessed sparked a desire to learn more. He began searching the internet and watching debates between Christians and Muslims. The information left him confused; he desperately wanted to know the truth but didn't know what to believe.

Ali's inner struggle often manifested as fits of rage. He recalls, "I would stay up all night, angry. I hated my dad, I hated my wife, and I hated my family." Observing this volatile behavior, James confronted him: "Why are you so angry?" Ali snapped back, "IT IS WHO I AM! Everyone around me is like this!"

Ali's turmoil would often boil over toward James. "He would call me in the middle of the night, screaming in anger," James remembers. "'You've stolen my dad from me! You owe us compensation because of all the persecution that has come down on my family!'"

James didn't back down. Able to see what was going on, he said, "Ali, I don't think I'm talking to you. It feels like I'm talking to a demon. The thoughts in your head are not from God; they're from Satan."

The truth hit Ali, and he fell silent, eventually saying, "I know. I have these evil thoughts in my head, and I don't know how to get rid of them."

James gave Ali a clear path to freedom: "You need to repent and believe in Jesus, make him your Lord, and get baptized."

Before his father, Ali confessed his anger, repented, and asked for forgiveness. In an act of humility and respect, he kissed his father's hands and feet and asked his father to baptize him. Ali's baptism purified him, and the next morning, he woke up a new man.

"The rage had left me," Ali says. "Now I love my dad. I respect him. I love my wife, and I love my children. I go to sleep early and wake up early, ready for work. My dad gave me a Bible, and I read it every day."

Just ten days later, his wife believed, and Ali baptized her. "Whatever I learn, I teach my wife," he explains. "Now my wife is sharing with her sister, and she is sharing with her husband."

Ali didn't stop with his family. He looked outward and started making disciples. He knew of villages in the mountains near the border with Syria that had never heard the gospel and had connections with influential people there. Despite the border skirmishes between Lebanon and Syria—with missiles and mortars falling—Ali was undeterred and went anyway.

On his mission, Ali met two Syrian refugees who were afraid of him because of his clan's reputation. However, he shared the gospel with them, and they listened. Aware of his family connections with crime, they asked, "Who are you?" Ali replied, "We are *Talamiz Al-Masih*—disciples of the Messiah. We love peace. We hate war. We're brothers. You can be my brother even though you're from Syria and I'm from Lebanon."

On another occasion, Ali visited a poor village. After he shared the gospel, one family believed, and Ali stayed to read the Bible with them for three hours. Then the conflict erupted again, and bombs fell nearby. Ali was forced to leave but plans to return once the fighting has stopped. "I'll bring Bibles with me," he says. "We'll stay in their house and continue the work."

Passing the Baton

As Ali matured in his faith, Ibrahim's wider family networks opened to the gospel. Ibrahim, with his connections everywhere, joined James on what James called a "modeling journey." Visiting Ibrahim's relatives near and far, they shared the gospel and the story of Zacchaeus (Luke 19:1–10). This story was ideal for Ibrahim's family networks: Not only is it a short, memorable account of grace and repentance, but it also ends by saying, "salvation has come to this house" (v.9), highlighting that when one family member followed Jesus, the door to faith was opened for the entire household. After sharing this message, family after family wanted to follow Jesus.

As a Westerner, it's no longer safe for James to travel with Ibrahim. However, this hasn't slowed the movement. Ibrahim led Jamal to Christ and trained him to lead. Together, they travel throughout the region, going from house to house. Now there are twelve families following Christ in Ibrahim's village and baptized disciples in one hundred other villages. Ibrahim and Jamal are out most days connecting with people and making disciples, aiming for a church in every village.

Ibrahim and Jamal are following a simple 4-Fields strategy.[2] They enter unreached areas seeking God-prepared people and households. They pray for needs and share the gospel. They gather disciples in groups to learn to obey what Christ has commanded and form new churches. They identify and develop leaders.

When a household believes, they begin working through a series of studies called the Commands of Christ, using 3-Thirds discipleship.[3] After baptism, they train and commission each new household to reach their community. Jamal and Ibrahim return to the villages and recruit a local leader to go with them and open new locations. Like the early church apostles Paul and Barnabas, they are building teams with their own Silas, Luke, Priscilla, and Aquila.

Jamal and Ibrahim train the next wave of workers to do what they do, using the simple MAWL approach James taught them: Model, Assist, Watch, and Launch.[4]

Today, they have trained twenty workers who go into unreached communities to:

- Share the gospel.
- Baptize new disciples.
- Teach them to obey Christ's commands.
- Gather as a church.
- Equip local leaders.

As the movement developed, James's role shifted, but his relationship with Ibrahim and Jamal remains the same. "We talk on the phone every day," James says. "We treat one another like family, even though Ibrahim is twice my age. I treat him like he's my father. His health isn't great, so I'll drive him to the doctor. Hope calls him to make sure he's okay and is taking his medication."

In the early days, James was more directive, but he admits that Ibrahim and Jamal are now more experienced in leading a movement than he is. He challenges Ibrahim and his leaders to find solutions for themselves in the Scriptures. One poignant example of this is when one of Ibrahim's disciples, a former Shia Muslim, died of cancer. Traditional Shia belief dictates specific rituals and Quranic prayers over the body, believed to help the deceased when they face judgment. Yet this man had died a follower of Christ, free and forgiven.

Ibrahim and Jamal asked James if they should allow the prayers.

Instead of answering, James pointed them to the Scriptures. They studied the parable of Lazarus and the Rich Man (Luke 16:19–31) and concluded that Muslim prayers couldn't harm this disciple, who was already with God. But they realized that three hundred Shia Muslims at the funeral needed to hear about Jesus. So they allowed Muslim prayers to be recited over the body, and then Ibrahim proclaimed the gospel to those attending, giving them a chance to repent before it was too late.

Troubleshooting

The movement's identity was tested when a militiaman arrived at the home of a disciple named Omar, a leader in a large and powerful clan, with many members who had recently turned to Christ. The militiaman threatened Omar and his family for following Jesus, then left. While the leaders were discussing how to respond, some of the younger men—still operating by the old clan code—took matters into their own hands.

They forced their way into the militiaman's house and told him, "You don't come to our leader's house uninvited! You don't threaten him and his family!" To emphasize their point, they broke his arm.

When Omar and the network leaders heard about this, their reaction was swift and countercultural. They found the young men and drove them to the hospital, where they apologized to the militiaman and paid his medical bills. Then they went to the man's home and apologized to his family. On the way home, the leaders told the young men, "What you did does not represent the Lord. If you do it again, we'll treat you like you're not followers of Jesus!"

Omar says this was the first time in history that anyone from his clan has asked for forgiveness from someone from the militiaman's clan. Only the gospel could have made that possible.

Like Peter in the garden waving his sword around (John 18:10), the young disciples were ready to fight, willing to go to jail, and prepared to defend the gospel—but in the wrong way. They learned a valuable lesson that night, and news of the unprecedented forgiveness spread throughout the entire region: These followers of the Messiah are a people who forgive.

Ibrahim believes that if they can reach their region, it will open the door to reaching their country. Already, the gospel is spreading through the disciples into other areas and other Arab lands. This is an Arab movement in a time of great turmoil, during which Muslims are seeking answers. Many are turning to Jesus, the Prince of Peace.

Cigarettes and Black Coffee

James and I left the city and drove across snow-covered mountains to meet with Ibrahim and his leaders. After passing through two military checkpoints, the empty shells of destroyed buildings served as a somber reminder of war. Before the day ended, a bomb fell just ten miles away.

For two hours, we sat in a smoke-filled room with seven leaders, drinking strong black coffee. Hearing these disciples of the Messiah speak of Isa was a wonder. Their accents, unique to Shia Muslims, differ from those of traditional Arab Christians. They know the Scriptures and talk of deep spiritual topics.

They come from rival clans that operate like drug cartels, yet their love for each other is real. Mustafa, for example, was a Sunni Muslim from Syria whose refugee camp was burned down by Lebanese Shia. Despite the old sectarian hatred, the disciples adopted him, loved him, and welcomed him to live among them.

Each reported on what God was doing in his field. They shared stories of how the gospel spread among their friends, family, and neighbors. New disciples were forming into churches. Over one hundred villages now have at least one church. There are nine streams of fourth-generation churches across the region.

All of this happened because God revealed himself to Ibrahim in a dream, and later, a car broke down outside his house, allowing a German missionary with no Arabic to see his misfortune as an opportunity to share the gospel.

We Plant and Water, but God Gives the Growth

Lebanon has been hard soil for centuries. Workers have labored for decades for a handful of new disciples. When James and Hope went out into a devastated community, they couldn't predict where it would lead. They followed the example of Jesus and the disciples he trained, trusting God for the outcome.

Reflect and Act

While the turmoil and triumphs faced by James, Hope, and Ibrahim are unique, the lessons that drove this movement's growth are universal. This is not just a story of war, forgiveness, and radical conversion; it's a profound example of how God works through dependence, simplicity, and local leadership.

This is a movement of God. The gospel goes out into unreached fields in the power of the Spirit through ordinary people. The messengers face impossible challenges, but wherever the gospel is preached, the result is disciples and churches to the glory of God.

To apply these lessons, this section challenges you to reflect on the movement dynamics presented in the story and to live them out in your own context.

As you reflect, remember the three essentials of a multiplying movement:

A movement's *Identity* mirrors the life and ministry of Jesus: obedient to the Word, dependent on the Holy Spirit, and faithful to the mission.

A movement's *Strategy* provides a clear path for expressing *Identity* in action—entering, gospeling, discipling, forming churches, and multiplying leaders.

A movement's *Methods* serve its *Strategy* and must be simple, effective, and contagious.

Movement Dynamics

Movements begin by finding the person of peace. The story started with James and Hope looking for God-prepared people. They found Leila, and through her, the gospel reached others. Through a German missionary, they met Ibrahim. Finding God-prepared insiders enabled the gospel to spread quickly through relational networks. The German's encounter with Ibrahim was a miracle, but it still required a *Strategy* and effort, as James and Hope invested in Ibrahim's growth as a disciple who makes disciples.

Movements prioritize obedience over perfection. James and Hope didn't wait until their Arabic was perfect; they stepped out in weakness and faith, offering prayer and the gospel, trusting God to open the way.

Movements can be catalyzed by outsiders. James acted as a careful master builder of disciples, churches, leaders, and movements. He modeled the *Strategy*, which included evangelism, making disciples, church formation, and leadership development. He knew it must be Ibrahim and other insiders who led this movement, not him.

Movements are driven by insiders. James and Hope started as outsiders. They learned the language and culture and connected with insiders like Ibrahim, who can reach their people. James practiced the MAWL (Model, Assist, Watch, and Launch) *Method* with Ibrahim, who, in turn, trained Jamal and other leaders to handle the rest. Most disciples in this movement don't even know who James is. Instead, ownership and leadership rests with the *Talamiz Al-Masih*—the disciples of the Messiah. Sitting around that smoke-filled room were seven men taking responsibility for the *Strategy*, as they monitored the health of the churches and the disciples and the spread of the gospel into new, unreached fields. A few years ago, they were nominal Shia Muslims with criminal backgrounds. It's not a movement unless insiders are driving it. If it's led by insiders, the chances of catalyzing movements in adjacent people groups are high.

***Movements rely on simple, reproducible* Methods.** James trained the disciples in best-practice principles and *Methods*. They made minor adjustments to accommodate the culture, but the *Strategy* and *Methods* remain similar to those used in other contexts. Using a 4-Fields *Strategy*, he trained them in the essentials and guided them in problem-solving, relying on the Bible as their authority.

Movements are fueled by changed lives that advance the gospel. At first, Ibrahim's family opposed his conversion, but he won them over through the power of a transformed life. Ibrahim turned away from anger, hatred, and violence. The Word and the Spirit shaped his *Identity*. He embraced love and forgiveness, winning the hearts of his people.

Movements expect persecution. Those who faithfully proclaim the gospel will face persecution. For these disciples, opposition comes from Islamic radicals, friends and family, and local police. Ibrahim and the disciples pay a price to follow Christ. Like in the book of Acts, respect in the community and persecution can happen simultaneously.

Movements recognize that God is Lord over history and the rulers of this world. God even uses humanity's rebellion to achieve his purposes. In his judgment, God may hand a people over to war and oppressive rule so that they turn to him. Evil appears to triumph. Empires rise. Injustice prevails, yet God has the final say.

Movements cascade movements. This movement began with one breakthrough, which led to the multiplication of disciples and churches. Now that it has started, it is spreading to nearby Arab-speaking, Muslim-background peoples.

Applying the Pattern

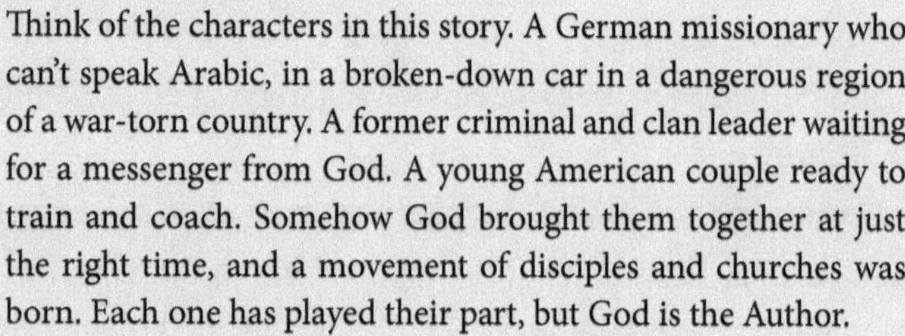

Reflect

Think of the characters in this story. A German missionary who can't speak Arabic, in a broken-down car in a dangerous region of a war-torn country. A former criminal and clan leader waiting for a messenger from God. A young American couple ready to train and coach. Somehow God brought them together at just the right time, and a movement of disciples and churches was born. Each one has played their part, but God is the Author.

Act

Read Acts 10 and fill out the 4-Fields Discovery worksheet in appendix one.

● How does Peter model each of these activities?

1. Enter unreached fields.
2. Share the gospel.
3. Train disciples.
4. Form churches.
5. Multiply leaders.

● How will you follow his example?

____

____

____

9

Sovereign Lord

Iran

And the word of God continued to increase, and the number of the disciples multiplied greatly.

ACTS 6:7 ESV

At Pentecost, the first believers included Persians, Parthians, and Medes (Acts 2:9). Since then, followers of Jesus have existed in the region now known as Iran.

When the Islamic revolution overthrew the Shah in 1979, Iran had a population of 39 million people, most of whom were Shia Muslims. On the eve of the revolution, the country held only five hundred Christians of Shia background. No one expected that the revolution would lead to a surge in conversions from Islam to Christ.[1] But God had a plan.

In 1969, Haik Hovsepian, a young pastor, started reaching out to Muslims.[2] The new disciples met in homes and spoke Persian (Farsi), rather than an ethnic Christian language like Armenian or Syriac. By 1976, twenty Muslim-background believers gathered in five churches.

Despite the hostile environment, Haik's ministry continued to expand. By 1981, the number of disciples had grown to sixty.[3]

The Islamic government demanded that Haik reveal the names of these Muslim-background believers, but he refused.

In 1993, Haik drew international attention to the plight of Mehdi Dibaj, whom the Islamic courts had imprisoned for over ten years for apostasy. The campaign embarrassed the government, and under international pressure, they released Mehdi. Three days later, Haik disappeared. Eventually, his body was found, riddled with stab wounds.[4]

The death of Haik Hovsepian sparked a fire across Iran. Hundreds of Muslim-background believers defied government agents—who were recording their names—to attend Haik's funeral.[5] A movement was forming.

The Insider

For centuries, Persians assumed that if anyone was a Christian, it was because they were born an Armenian or an Assyrian. Not anymore. Today, approximately 1.5 million followers of the Messiah Jesus are in Iran.[6] Diar is one of them.

From his earliest years, Diar was immersed in the rigorous routines of his Islamic faith, observing the five daily prayers, attending the mosque, and fasting during Ramadan. His father, hoping Diar would become an Imam, sent him to study Arabic and the Quran. When Diar found contradictions in the Islamic scriptures, he pressed his teacher for an explanation, who simply responded, "This is the Word of God. You must obey."

In his heart, Diar could not submit to such blind obedience.

As a Kurdish Iranian, Diar had experienced the regime's mistreatment of its people. Wanting to leave Islam behind, he started exploring other faiths, praying, "God, I want to know you! Who are you? Are you there? If you're good, why is there so much evil in the world?" After four years of intense searching, he found nothing. Disillusioned, he became an atheist and joined the Communist resistance against the regime. He felt empty and angry.

Then one night, he had a powerful dream. He saw a shining light over the mountains and heard people calling out, "Jesus is coming!" The light revealed that each person had an inner darkness that controlled them, making them deaf and blind slaves. Seeing the darkness within himself, he was afraid.

When Diar woke, he began his search for Jesus. He knew the Quran acknowledged Jesus as a prophet, but he needed to learn more. Since visiting a church could get him imprisoned, he traveled across the border to Kurdish Iraq to find a church and learn about Jesus. There, he visited a house church, and they shared the gospel with him. Diar repented, put his faith in Jesus, and was baptized. Later, he returned to Iran, aiming to show others that they too could be forgiven and released from the darkness within.

He proclaimed God's Word with power, talking to everyone he knew and seeing people set free by Jesus. As individuals were healed, forgiven, and delivered from demons, the Word spread. However, the opposition from the government and radical Muslims intensified just as quickly. It became increasingly difficult for Diar to conceal his activities, so he fled the country and waited for the persecution to subside.

"Despite the danger, I still wanted to reach my people and my nation," Diar says. "Yet I didn't know how. I prayed that God would lead me to the right people." His prayer was answered when God brought an outsider into his story.

The Outsider

When Jerry and his family arrived in northern Iraq, he was already an experienced movement catalyst. He had spent two

years in North India training and coaching leaders among the
Bhojpuri and Magahi peoples, resulting in multiple streams of
new disciples and churches. Their progress drew the attention of
the authorities, and Jerry was deported.

Northern Iraq was a war zone at the time, with the Kurds
fighting ISIS. Amid this crisis, Jerry worked among the displaced
populations, focusing on the Syrian refugees and internally
displaced Iraqi Kurds. He discipled them and trained them to
establish churches. It was during this work that Jerry met Diar,
who had crossed the border from Iran into Iraq with friends
who had recently come to faith. He wanted them baptized and
discipled so they could learn how to follow Jesus.

In India, Jerry had learned some simple, biblical skills and
tools for reaching unreached communities, sharing the gospel,
making disciples, forming churches, and multiplying leaders. He
trained Diar in these strategies and methods, telling him, "We're
not baptizing any more of your people. We'll train you. You go
back and baptize them, train disciples, and form healthy churches
that multiply."

With this shift, Diar's one-man ministry was becoming a
movement.

He continued to bring leaders across the border for training.
Their study focused on two key areas: the traits of godly leaders
found in the books of Timothy and Titus, and the priesthood of
every believer—recognizing the authority Jesus gave to share the
gospel, baptize, make disciples, and plant churches.

As the trainees studied Revelation chapters 7 and 9–10, God
worked on their identity, helping them to understand that their
task was to help reach the multitude from "every nation, tribe,
people and language" (Revelation 7:9). This translated into a bold
vision to reach new locations, people groups, and provinces—a

vision they immediately implemented among their families and communities.

One of the leaders trained across the border was Roya, a professional whose work required her to travel across different Iranian provinces. After the training, she returned home and trained her family and friends. Sixty-nine of them now meet in thirteen churches and discipleship groups across three provinces.

Jerry and Diar followed up by teaching Roya the characteristics of a healthy church (Acts 2:36–47).[7] When they asked her which one needed attention, she responded, "We need to get all the new disciples baptized!" This became her focus, and she completed the tasks within a week, using baths and kiddie pools!

Diar recognizes the foundational role of the training he has received: "We couldn't have done it without the training, coaching, love, and support from Jerry and others. He has released everything to us—he teaches us, and then we do it and train others. We teach, we baptize, we help disciples start churches."

Jerry only sees the leaders for a short time when they cross the border. "It's essential to teach them to find their identity by abiding in Christ," he says. "That's where the fruit comes from. They share the Jesus they have met. The Lord is moving. He is multiplying his disciples and churches in Iran."

Forming Churches

When the Iranian churches gather, they follow the pattern of Acts 2. They study the Word, pray for one another, worship together, share their highs and lows, celebrate the Lord's Supper, and give generously.

Their method for studying the Word is highly practical and involves asking:

- What does this passage tell us about God and his character?
- What does this tell us about people and their character?
- Are there sins I need to avoid or confess?
- How can I obey what we've learned this week?

Through prayer and encouragement, believers spur one another to follow Christ and make disciples. Diar explains their simple strategy: "Each disciple reaches the people around them with simple methods for sharing the gospel, making disciples, and planting churches that reproduce."

The network has grown to around two thousand churches across twenty-six of Iran's thirty-one provinces. Some streams have reached twelve generations of churches. To minimize the risk of attracting attention, these churches typically have about four or five people.

Local elder-pastors have been appointed to lead the streams. Others act as apostolic catalysts, providing training, coaching, and entering new fields. Individual churches maintain relationships with the church that started them and the ones they establish. However, it's not safe for them to be in contact with all the other churches within the streams.

This work comes at a cost. Disciples have been arrested and interrogated, and one person has been killed.

The Journey to Faith

After interviewing Diar and his wife, Nadia, online, I wanted to meet them and their coworkers in person. Because meeting in Iran was too dangerous, we arranged to rendezvous in a Muslim country in the Middle East, where there would be less scrutiny. They were already traveling there for training, presenting the ideal opportunity to conduct multiple in-depth interviews with them and their leaders.

The apartment where we met was filled with the sound of the Muslim call to prayer, echoing through the city five times a day. The leaders I spoke with were all relatively new believers, having followed Christ for less than five years. Yet, each had between thirty and over one hundred churches in their streams of multiplication. These streams represent just a single network within a movement of God sweeping across the Islamic Republic—an unprecedented development in the 1,400 years since Islam conquered Persia.

Here are some of the recurring themes they shared that help us understand how God is at work.

Disillusionment

Some grew up in very religious homes, while others had never seen their parents reading the Quran or praying. Regardless, they all went to schools that enforced Islam through threats and intimidation. These Farsi speakers had to learn to recite the Quran in Arabic and rigidly follow required prayers and fasts. On the surface, they obeyed; inside, they rebelled.

Long before they heard of Christ, their hearts had grown cold toward their inherited faith. More than disillusionment, there was anger. This generation of Iranians has largely turned its back on Islam, maintaining only the outward appearance necessary to avoid trouble with the authorities.

These Iranians don't want Christians to use the Quran as a bridge to the gospel, as is common in some outreach strategies to Muslims. They've already rejected the Quran and its system; they're ready to hear about Jesus.

A Crisis

Iranians face the same struggles we do—health crises, financial insecurities, marriage breakdowns, bouts of depression, and the loss of loved ones. Life happens, and these issues shake all of us to the core, prompting questions such as, "Why is this happening?" or "How do I get through this time?" Many Iranians turn to God, hoping they are not alone. In desperation, they pray. But they are not praying to the god of Islam.

One disciple, Mahsa, moved in with her grandparents during her teens after her parents divorced, an experience that left her feeling empty. Her husband, Arash, struggled with depression and was frequently out of work due to economic sanctions against the regime. Compounding their stress, their son needed urgent medical treatment, which they could not afford.

When a relative shared the gospel with Mahsa, she accepted Christ. Arash could see the change in her but wasn't sure he could commit. Then, while their son was being prepared for surgery, Arash received a message confirming a job offer from a company in Europe. Overwhelmed, he fell to his knees, crying and acknowledging that God had intervened.

The Search

Unmoored from Islam, many start searching for answers. Some go to the library; others browse the internet. One man asked his uncle, who lived overseas, to send him a Bible in Farsi. Another read a Bible he borrowed from an Armenian Christian. Others watch movies about Jesus on smuggled DVDs. Omid bought a DVD featuring the Kurdish warrior Saladin, only to discover that it was about the life of Jesus. Many are impressed when they learn that Jesus was a man of peace who died a violent death for the world's sin and rose again.

Signs Along the Way

Remarkably, about one in four people I interviewed had a dream that led them to Jesus. Yasmin dreamt of a massive mountain with a figure of light pointing to a cross on a lake. She then heard a crowd of thousands calling her to move toward the sign. Others recall powerful childhood memories: As a boy, Amir visited an old church building and saw a painting of Jesus and Mary. He felt a deep peace, which he didn't understand at the time but couldn't forget. Another man treasured a cross, given to him as jewelry by a beloved uncle, and eventually wanted to understand its meaning.

Someone They Trust

Universally, the final breakthrough happens when someone they love and trust takes the risk to share. A cousin, a colleague, a husband, or a wife sits them down and explains the gospel, sharing how Jesus has changed their life. They then challenge them to repent, believe, be baptized, and follow him.

One name kept resurfacing: Nadia, Diar's wife. For many people in the room, Nadia had been the starting point. Amin told me, "I was very desperate. I had financial problems and family issues when Nadia shared the gospel with my wife and me. We've known her since childhood, and I trust her with all my heart. So, the moment she shared the gospel with us, we both accepted it. Now we're doing for others what she did for us."

Invariably, the gospel spreads as new disciples begin to witness to their inner circles, but they must navigate this with caution. Sharing their faith often carries significant personal risk, especially for those whose parents are strict Muslims. However, God's timing can overcome those hurdles. For example, one disciple kept his faith a secret from his devout mother. It wasn't until a health crisis shook the entire family that the opportunity arose. In her desperation, the mother's heart became receptive to the gospel. She turned and believed, and the son had the privilege of baptizing his own mother.

My enduring memory of these Iranians is a powerful reminder of their freedom. As our time together concluded, they formed a circle, linked hands, and sang and danced for joy, knowing the next day they would return to the dangers of Iran. By the time their flight touched down, the women would be out of sight again, covered once more by their hijabs.

This Is God's Story, but We Have a Part to Play

God in his wisdom has shaken the Muslim world, and there is unprecedented openness to the gospel. We can't control when or how he does that, but we can be ready wherever we are in the world. We can be in the field connecting with people far from God, sharing the gospel, making disciples, planting churches, multiplying leaders, even when progress is slow and hard.

Reflect and Act

God is at work in the complexity of Iran's history. The story is unique, but the lessons are universal. To apply these lessons, this section challenges you to reflect on the movement dynamics presented in the story and to live them out in your own context.

As you reflect, remember the three essentials of a multiplying movement:

A movement's *Identity* mirrors the life and ministry of Jesus: obedient to the Word, dependent on the Holy Spirit, and faithful to the mission.

A movement's *Strategy* provides a clear path for expressing *Identity* in action—entering, gospeling, discipling, forming churches, and multiplying leaders.

A movement's *Methods* serve its *Strategy* and must be simple, effective, and contagious.

Movement Dynamics

Movements trust God's sovereignty. This is central to their *Identity*. Who would have predicted that God's plan for Iran was to hand the country over to Islamists? Yet, he is shaping human history to fulfill his purposes. He turns what people intend for evil into good.

After the revolution, the Islamist strategy was to stop Christianity from spreading from Armenian and Syrian communities into the Farsi-speaking majority. They banned the Farsi Bible, outlawed Christian gatherings in Farsi, and forbade Muslims from attending. Muslims who followed Jesus were threatened with imprisonment and death; some, like Haik Hovsepian, paid the ultimate price.

Yet, the government's use of coercion weakened its legitimacy, exposing the truth of God's power in Christ.[8] The regime's credibility was further diminished by its failures. Because the government claimed to rule according to god's laws, not man's, when the regime failed militarily, politically, and economically, Islam was discredited.[9]

Advances in technology prevented the regime from stopping

the flow of information from Christian sources. When millions of Iranians fled the regime and settled abroad, many found Christ and shared their newfound faith with friends and family back home.

The Ayatollahs seized power and eliminated all rivals. They maintained control through the strength of the State, supported by the Revolutionary Guards and the police. Despite their monopoly on power, they could not stop the growth of this "powerless" community.[10] Islam had power, but it had lost its legitimacy.

The message of a crucified Carpenter, who is the victorious and eternal King of Kings (a Persian title), is resonating with Iranians weary of the oppressive control of a discredited religion.[11]

God is Creator and Lord of history, and the future belongs to him!

Applying the Pattern

Reflect

As Iran was about to fall to the Islamic Revolution, Haik Hovsepian, pioneer and martyr, was preparing the way for a movement of God that would sweep the nation. No one expected or predicted this could happen. God chooses ordinary people like Haik, Diar, and Nadia to play their part in his unfolding story. What part has he called you to play?

Act

Read Acts 4:23–31.

- How does a movement respond to the pressure to remain silent?
- How will you resist the pressure and freely share the good news about Jesus?

Conclusion

Worth the Risk

The movement of God is evident in the book of Acts. Neither the early church nor its leaders are the main characters. The central figure is God the Father, Son, and Holy Spirit, who initiates, sustains, and completes his mission. It's his story, but we have a part to play. What Jesus began to do in the Gospels, the risen Lord continues today, as the Word spreads in the power of the Spirit through ordinary people. The fruit is disciples and churches to God's glory. Everywhere.

The stories detailed throughout this book—from the bombed-out cities of the Middle East to the prisons of Texas and the remote villages of Laos—reveal that the movement of God is not a thing of the past but a present, unstoppable reality.

Jesus Leads the Way

These movements are not defined by complexity or large, centralized institutions but by their alignment with the life and ministry of Jesus, characterized by the three elements of *Identity*, *Strategy*, and *Methods*.

Identity

The heart of every movement is transformed disciples, whose *Identity* is rooted in surrender to God's Word, dependence on the Holy Spirit, and faithfulness to the core missionary task.

The movements we've read about operate under the authority of God's living Word. It is the same Word that brought the universe into existence. It is this same power that invades a prison cell and sets a captive free. It is the power that transforms a student, a farmer, a criminal, and a widow into catalysts for a nationwide movement. And it is the power that breaks through the impossible by using vivid dreams and powerful childhood memories to draw individuals to Jesus.

Disciples are equipped with the Word, going from door to door, village to village, cell to cell, and suburb to suburb, offering prayer, a simple gospel outline, and inviting people to read the Bible together. They go in the power of the Spirit, who bears witness to the Lord Jesus through their weakness.

In Lebanon, the Spirit told Ibrahim a messenger was on the way. He waited, and soon after, a German missionary's car broke down right outside his home. The German couldn't speak Arabic, and Ibrahim couldn't speak German, yet through God's power, this unlikely meeting sparked a movement.

In Indonesia, Arif, disillusioned, cut off all contact with the field. But the Spirit continued working. Ten months later, Arif returned and reconnected with Joyo and all the new disciples. God had profoundly transformed Arif's heart in the wilderness.

The Spirit led James and Hope into a bombed-out Lebanese city, where they offered prayer in basic Arabic. God used this to reach Leila, whose faith in Christ was just the beginning of something far greater.

These movements thrive in hostile environments, often under the oppressive rule of Islamists, Communists, Hindu nationalists, and criminal gangs. They refuse to be silenced, choosing prison or even death over compromise.

Whatever the context, movements are made up of groups of disciples who gather around the Word, learning to obey what their Lord has commanded. The Word is in the hands and hearts of God's people.

Their mission is clear and non-negotiable: disciples and churches to the glory of God. Everywhere. They meticulously map their progress, tracking generations of disciples, churches, and leaders, and engage the gaps they identify.

Strategy

A clear *Strategy* turns *Identity* into action, ensuring each disciple has a part to play.

Movements enter unreached fields. Movements leave the ninety-nine to find the one. In Lebanon, Ibrahim and Jamal don't wait for people to come to them; they go to them. They visit homes, praying for needs and sharing the gospel in a Muslim region. Movements look for God-prepared people—people of peace—who open the door into entire communities. A roadside stop for chai was Ravi's chance to connect with the owner and see if he wanted a return visit. Ravi leads by example, but he knows he is not the solution for India; instead, he focuses his energy on training thousands of everyday disciples to turn a cup of chai into a conversation about Jesus and an invitation to read the Bible.

Movements share the gospel. They are not ashamed of the good news. Sometimes it's shared upfront and early; other times, it follows a series of Bible studies. But sooner or later, everyone encounters the gospel. The disciples in Laos trained thousands across the country, ensuring everyone knew what to say and do. As a result, almost a quarter of a million people there heard the gospel person-to-person in 2024. In Rajasthan, India, eight out of ten disciples are actively making disciples, visiting relatives and friends, and riding buses to remote, unreached villages. In Texas, every prisoner who turns to Christ is immediately taught to pass on the gospel. That's what movements do.

Movements make disciples. In Acts, Luke doesn't count "decisions"; he tracks the number of baptized disciples added to the community (Acts 2:41). In these movements, becoming a disciple is not about raising a hand or bowing a head to say a prayer. Instead, it's about obeying Christ's command to repent, believe, and be baptized for the forgiveness of sins (Acts 2:38). The person who brings someone to Christ is the one who typically baptizes them. Then, the new disciple joins a group and learns to obey what Jesus commanded. As soon as possible, someone will coach them to start their own group.

In Lebanon, Ibrahim was the first disciple in his clan. James trained him to make disciples. When two relatives turned to Christ, James baptized the first one and then showed Ibrahim how to baptize the next. Ibrahim, not James, taught them how to follow Christ; in a movement, there is no such thing as a "mature" disciple who is not making disciples.

Movements form churches. Making disciples and establishing churches are two inseparable sides of the same coin. You can't do one without the other. In California, as Troy and Rick discipled Shane, they discovered that he was a person of peace. They cast a vision for the kind of community Shane knew his friends and family needed, and, with their support, he gathered the new disciples and started a church.

Acts 2:36–47 serves as the guide for healthy discipleship and thriving churches. Not all elements may be present from the beginning, but they point toward the destination.

During my time in India, we held church in the courtyard. The heat was relentless, and noisy fans struggled to keep up. There, as we sang, worshipped, shared, and obeyed God's Word, I realized I could have been in Lebanon, Ghana, or a Texas prison. The language, architecture, and local customs were different, but the pattern was the same—simple and powerful. The Word and the Spirit were at work in the hearts of God's people, with no distractions. This is the core of a movement.

Movements multiply leaders. Every new disciple is trained as a worker who can share the gospel and make disciples. This creates an environment where leaders emerge who can not only make disciples and plant churches but also multiply them.

In Lebanon, Jamal and Ibrahim regularly return to the villages with new disciples and recruit a local leader to go with them and open new locations. They have trained twenty workers who go into unreached communities to share the gospel, baptize new disciples, teach them to obey Christ's commands, and gather as a church. They use the MAWL (Model, Assist, Watch, and Launch) method to train them.[1]

The emerging apostolic leaders are not known for their platform ministry or the size of their audience. Instead, they are recognized for making disciples, planting churches, and developing leaders. Volunteers, not professionals, lead local churches. Limited funding is available for those who have already demonstrated their ability to multiply healthy churches and reach unreached fields.

Methods

Movements utilize simple, transferable *Methods*. In two case studies, we saw how microSD cards loaded with text and audio Bibles transformed steady progress into rapid growth, both in depth and breadth. The best *Methods* are born of an uncompromising vision that demands field trials and feedback.

When Troy met Max at the skatepark in California, he knew

what steps to take. He trained Max in simple tools, including the 411, 3-Thirds discipleship, the Commands of Christ, MAWL, and the Church Circle.[2] Max was a natural evangelist, but Troy equipped him with simple *Methods* that made him more effective at making disciples. Max then took those *Methods* and skills to Phoenix and multiplied disciples and churches.[3]

Methods alone can't create a movement, but simple, proven ones amplify and deepen its impact.

You Have a Part to Play

It's not within our power to engineer a movement. God's sovereignty governs history. He raises nations and brings them down. He opens doors and closes them. In Iran, for example, it was God who handed that nation over to Islamic rule—a generation later, thousands are turning to Christ.

The times are wholly in God's hands. Yet we have a part to play. Our job is to take his Word, in the power of the Spirit, to a lost world. The risen Lord restored his disciples by returning them to the Word of God, reminding them of the core missionary task, and providing the gift of the Spirit. He does the same for us.

He Is Worth It

The work is hard, the cost is high, and the fight is real. In Ghana, Terry and Amy Ruff faced life-threatening cancer, home invasions, and leadership failure. They held on to Jesus' promise that he will always be with them.

In India, it took seven years of hard work before the final breakthrough came. The team persevered even when it seemed like nothing was "working."

Though authorities murdered Chantha's husband in Laos,

she heard the call of God to continue the work among her people. What was once impossible, God has accomplished through her. What Satan intended for destruction, God has used to bring salvation. Through pain and loss, God shaped the heart of a woman of God.

Jai spent over a year in prison and received death threats from officials in Laos. Yet, despite having a young family, he refused to abandon his calling, continuing to plant hundreds of churches and seeing thousands turn to Christ. Jai chooses to risk all because he knows Jesus is worth it.

Stories like this point to a movement of God: the abandoned widow, now a respected leader and catalyst for others; the young man cursed by the gods, now rescued from despair; the fathers in India, now sober, hardworking, loving their families, and making disciples near and far.

Follow Me, and I'll Teach You

Not everyone is called to Iraq, Laos, or the Texas prisons. Still, every disciple of Jesus has been given the commission to follow him and make disciples. He promises that he will teach us how to fish for people (Matthew 4:19). Movements don't only happen in dangerous places—they can happen in your own backyard.

You might be wondering how these global principles can apply to your life and ministry. Perhaps we can learn from how God disrupted one New Zealand couple and took them in a totally new direction.

Nick and Sarah Field had achieved significant ministry success, serving as pastors for twenty-five years at a church in Wellington, New Zealand, which grew to over a thousand people meeting in four congregations.[4]

Yet God was calling them to something new—and from their

story we can learn how God realigns us to play our part in multiplying movements. Everywhere.

1. ***When God disrupts you, lean in.*** Nick and Sarah's journey began with the 2020 lockdown, which unsettled their established twenty-five-year rhythm and compelled them to step back from their successful ministry.

2. ***Ask the right questions.*** During the lockdown, they took the time to ask: What does the Great Commission look like for us here in New Zealand? How do we make disciples who make disciples?

3. ***Look for answers in the right place.*** They studied the Gospel of Mark and the Acts of the Apostles, reading each chapter aloud. They found they couldn't get through a chapter without bursting into tears; the Holy Spirit broke them. They read, they cried, they prayed.

4. ***Let God's Word question your experience.*** As they read God's Word, they began to realize that what they saw in Scripture was different from what they had experienced in ministry. The Spirit began to show them that there were patterns and principles they needed to pursue. Instead of bringing Scripture down to their level, they allowed Scripture to question their experience.

5. ***Step out of the boat.*** A year later, with the church's blessing, they resigned as pastors and began pursuing movements of disciples and churches. They left behind what they knew and moved into an uncertain future, trusting that God had a plan. Over the next eighteen months, they trained people across New Zealand to be churches that make disciples in their communities,

planting four churches in their city and initiating a nationwide network.

6. ***Find your tribe.*** Nick and Sarah didn't go alone. God connected them with others in New Zealand and around the world on the same journey—some ahead, some behind, some alongside.

7. ***Follow the fruit.*** Nick and Sarah's prayer-walking in their street led to a breakthrough, with neighbors becoming disciples who make disciples. This included Justine, who led Vesna to Christ and into the church community. The chain reaction continued as Vesna shared the gospel with her family in Serbia. Now she meets with them weekly online to tell them what she is learning, and is planning a trip to Serbia to train them. Nick and Sarah's vision is to see stories of multiplication repeated in every region of New Zealand.

Do you want to experience your own stories of transformation and movement? The time to start is now, and the best place is right where you are. Our Master has entrusted us with resources. He will return one day to judge the world and put things right. He's placed some gold coins in your pocket. What will you do with them?

Deeper Studies

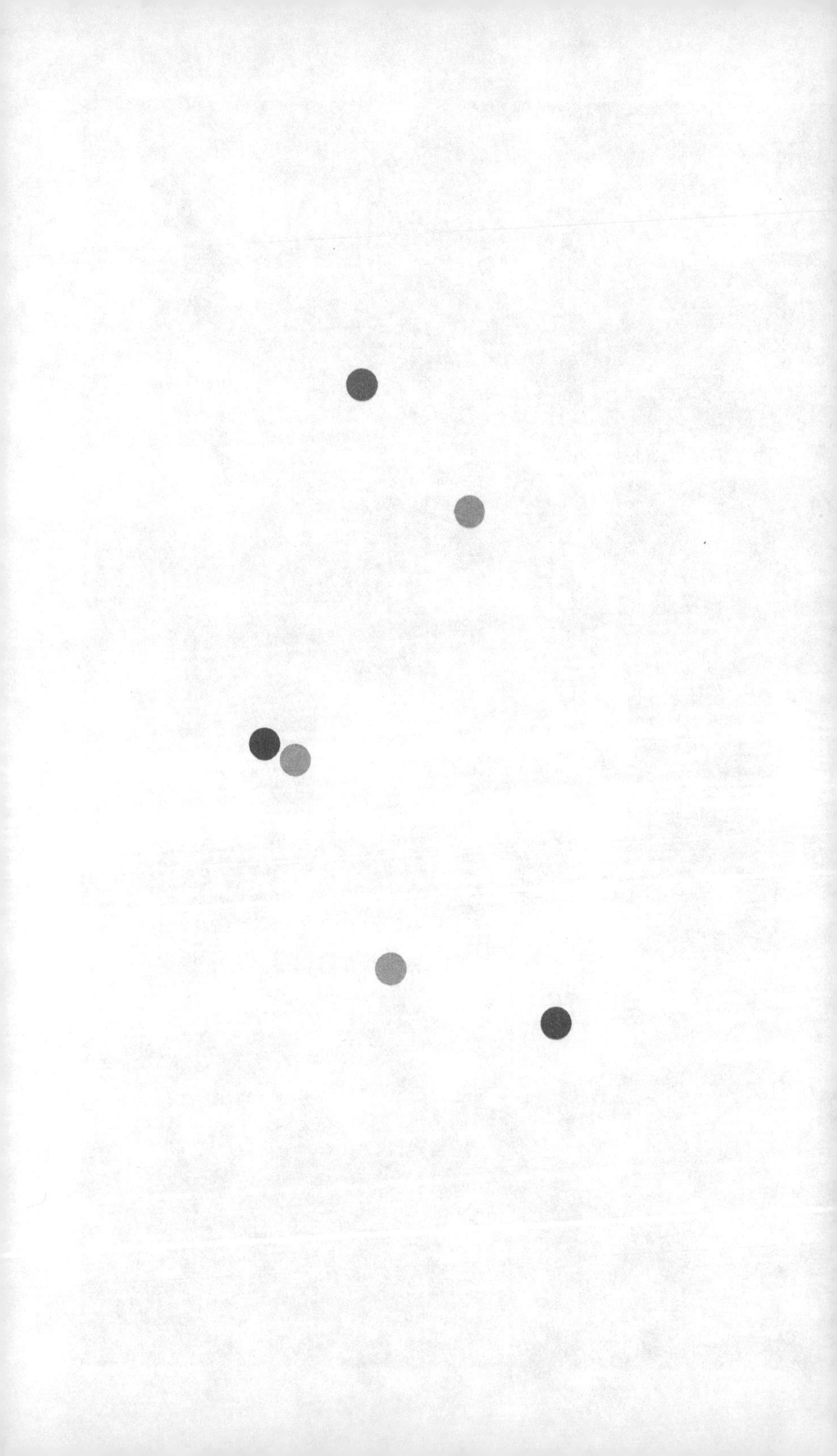

Deeper Studies

1

Deeper

How God Shapes Movement Leaders

When Jesus called his first disciples, he didn't just give them a job; he gave them a new identity (Luke 5:4–11). His call to follow him was a command that defined who they were—requiring obedience and surrender—before it defined what they did. He also promised to teach them how to fish for people, so that they would be equipped for the mission. Jesus' example shows us how God shapes leaders throughout their lives in two distinct yet inseparable ways:

- Who we are—character and spiritual formation.
- What we do—ministry formation.

Sometimes, God allows the process of formation to take place through extreme pressure and unexpected trials. Why did God allow Paul to be in chains on a sinking ship during a hurricane (Acts 27)? There must have been an easier way to get him to Rome. But God isn't interested in the easiest or quickest results. Instead, God allowed the crisis to refine and validate Paul's faith before a watching world. As the leader of a multiplying movement, his character and faith were tested by this life-and-death crisis. He was learning, once again, how to trust God before he continued in his mission.

In Indonesia, Arif answered God's call to resign as a pastor and focus on making disciples among the unreached. The Spirit guided him to an area where he and Joyo worked diligently but saw little fruit. Arif, deeply discouraged, walked away. However, God brought him back months later and revealed the fruit that had begun to sprout in his absence. Arif and Joyo worked hard, but it was God who caused the growth. God refined Arif's heart and taught him profound truths about his identity—lessons that are best learned in obscurity—before God brought visible success. In his time, God clarified the strategy and methods, and the movement began to grow, led by Arif, whom God could now trust with success.

Today, Arif oversees a movement of 125,000 disciples.

In India, Gary and Ravi persisted for seven years in the field, searching for the most effective methods. But it wasn't just a practical exercise. Their partnership, faith, and commitment grew. God shaped their hearts. When the breakthroughs came, they knew it was God who had been with them all along. They could be trusted with a multiplying movement because they had been tested and they persevered.

Sometimes, when I train leaders in movement principles, they exclaim, "Why didn't we know this ten years ago! Imagine how much further ahead we'd be now." I remind them that the right strategy and methods are not enough. For years, God has been shaping their identity, preparing them for these breakthroughs.

I think of Chantha, Noy's widow in Laos, a woman of faith. Though her suffering could have bred bitterness, she turned to Christ in her pain and responded to his call to carry on Noy's work. This kind of character and faith doesn't drop out of a manual; it's forged in the fire. Chantha trains, practices, and mentors others using effective strategies, with the authority of a woman dedicated to God.

This is a rapidly growing movement that has increased from three thousand to over ten thousand disciples, without taking shortcuts.

Even for the most seasoned leaders, this reshaping of who they are is a lifelong process, initiated by God. Consider Peter, the leader of the Twelve, who stood hesitating in the doorway of Cornelius's house (Acts 10; 11:1–18). It had been ten years since Jesus commanded him and the disciples to go to the nations, yet Peter's character and cultural background prevented him from executing that part of the ministry mandate. Aside from a few exceptions, there was no Gentile mission.

Peter was an apostle, trained by Jesus, filled with the Spirit, and he had already planted the first church in Jerusalem. Yet God had to intervene to shape Peter's heart and mind. This should encourage us. This is a movement of God, not a movement of Peter, Paul, or you and me. God takes the initiative to shape and redirect even the most mature leaders, including Peter. We should expect the same and embrace it.

Read Acts 27; 28:1–10.

- What do we learn about God from this story?

- What do we learn about people?

- What do we learn about how God shapes movement leaders?

- What do you need to do to obey what you've learned?

2

Deeper

What Do Movements Do?

The movements in these pages have a singular focus on multiplying disciples and churches to the glory of God. Everywhere.

They express their mission in concrete activities, not abstractions. They train every disciple to make disciples and form healthy churches. Everyone knows what to do on Monday morning.

In contrast, for the last hundred years, Westerners have been redefining the nature of God's mission in the world. Driven by a confidence in human potential, "mission" has increasingly been framed in political, economic, and social terms. This focus implies a universalism that questions the judgment of a holy God. Why seek to save the lost if we no longer believe anyone is truly lost? Under this framework, sin is not the problem; the problem is the dehumanizing structures of society.

Whenever Western Christians have turned political and social transformation into the core missionary task while neglecting the Great Commission, the result has always been decline and decay.[1] The New Testament does not promise the transformation of society in this life. Jesus' mission was met with opposition at every level. The people of Nazareth, who knew Jesus best, were the ones who tried to kill him (Luke 4:29). Capernaum, where Jesus spent so much time, faced judgment. They saw the miracles, they heard the teaching, and yet they would not turn (Matthew 11:21–24). Jerusalem was not transformed but must await the judgment of God (Matthew

23:37–39). Paul's ministry was no different. None of the cities he visited were transformed—disrupted, yes, but not transformed. Instead, as the Word spread, in every place, the Spirit formed those who repented and believed into the new people of God who were witnesses to the ends of the earth.[2] That is what movements do.

God is the chief character in the book of Acts, and his Word propels the story forward.[3] Angels appear, prophets speak, prison doors open, houses shake, thousands believe, persecutors fall to the ground, the Scriptures are fulfilled. God directs his mission. At the center of this mission is the witness to the life, death, and victory of Jesus, calling everyone to turn and believe in him and leading to the formation of communities of disciples everywhere.

Texas prisons *are* changing, but as a byproduct of a disciple making movement. When a black brother baptizes a former white supremacist, it is the overflow of a movement of God. This is not a prison reform initiative; it is a disciple making movement.

In a Lebanese region where Islamists and criminal clans vie for control, the gospel goes out and often brings blessing. Yet social transformation is not guaranteed; persecution is just as likely.

In India, husbands and wives are reconciled. In Laos, a widow forgives the officials who ordered her husband's murder. Both are the result of a movement of God that multiplies disciples and churches. Transformation is a *fruit* of the gospel, but it's not guaranteed. Jesus told his disciples they would be persecuted, and that's what multiplying movements typically experience.

Their hope is not in the transformation of this world but in Christ and the new world to come on the other side of God's judgment. Until then, we have Jesus' assurance that "repentance for the forgiveness of sins will be preached in his name to all nations" (Luke 24:47). That's what movements do.

Read Matthew 28:16–20.

● What do we learn about God from this story?

____

____

____

● What do we learn about people?

____

____

____

● What do we learn about the core missionary task?

____

____

____

● What do you need to do to obey what you've learned?

____

____

3

Deeper

The Battle

A body, brutally murdered, was found by the side of the road in Laos. This tragedy did not have to happen. If Noy had only stopped speaking about Jesus, he would still be alive today. Yet Noy knew that the battle was worth the cost. When his widow, Chantha, with five children to raise, heard God's call to continue her husband's work, a great victory was won. This is spiritual warfare at its finest; not just prayer but the prayer of surrender at the very moment when nothing makes sense.

Jesus faced that same battle. Satan tempted Jesus to betray his Sonship and his mission. Tired, alone, and hungry, Jesus won his fight in the wilderness by surrendering to his Father's Word and remaining faithful to his mission. Then he marched into Galilee in the power of the Spirit, casting out demons, healing the sick, and proclaiming the gospel (Luke 4:1–14).

The movement is born out of battle and born for battle. The Gospels and Acts reveal how Satan attacked and undermined every new stage in God's plan of salvation. He sifted the disciples like wheat and inspired Judas to betray Jesus.[1] Satan's purpose is to snatch away the Word of God so that people do not believe and are not saved (Luke 8:11–12). Jesus won his battle against Satan through obedience to his Father's Word, dependence on the Holy Spirit, and faithfulness to his mission to lay down his life as a ransom for many. He won the victory, but the battle rages until the end. Jesus enlisted his disciples in the battle and shared his power and authority over the Enemy.

In Acts, when Satan stirred up the rulers of this world to destroy the movement, Jesus' disciples prayed for the power of the Spirit and boldness to proclaim the Word (Acts 4:23–31). The victory over Satan was tangibly demonstrated by the establishment of disciples and churches learning to obey Jesus.

Today, the attacks come in many forms. Family rejection. Fruitless years. Team conflict. False accusations and imprisonment. It's in the darkest places that the battle is fought and won, when we have nothing left, yet cling to Christ. There is no greater weapon in our warfare. The fiercer the attack, the more we trust and obey. This is how victory is won—alone in the storm with nothing left except God's faithfulness.

Terry and Amy Ruff learned this when God called them to Ghana. Over fourteen years, they faced life-threatening cancer, criminal violence, and leadership moral failure. They clung to Christ and continued the work. In and through their weakness, God brought victory.

Satan aims to destroy faith in God's Word, which alone brings salvation. The key weapon in Jesus' arsenal was his surrender to the Father's will.

Revelation reminds us, "They triumphed over Satan by the blood of the Lamb and by the word of their testimony; they did not love their lives so much as to shrink from death" (12:11). This is the way of the cross. This is how the battle is won.

Read Ephesians 6:10–20.

● What do we learn about God from this story?

____

____

____

● What do we learn about people?

____

____

____

● What do we learn about the battle?

____

____

____

● What do you need to do to obey what you've learned?

____

____

____

4
Deeper

Movements and Persecution

Both prophecy and persecution marked the life of Jesus, a pattern he taught his followers to expect. Simeon prophesied over the infant Jesus that he would divide Israel (Luke 2:34–35). This opposition began early, when Jesus was rejected in his hometown of Nazareth, grew throughout his mission, and culminated in his death in Jerusalem.

Jesus taught his disciples to expect persecution not just as a sign of the very end of time but of the present age. New believers today can be rejected by their families and thrown out of their homes, mirroring the experience Jesus faced in his town. Persecution can also come from authorities. For example, in India, Hindu nationalists often accuse Christians of forced or induced conversions and pressure the police to investigate. Though these accusations are eventually proven false, Christians are punished in the meantime through interrogation, threats, temporary imprisonment, and trial.

Elsewhere, in Laos, Communist officials warn leaders to stop taking the gospel to new villages and people groups. Failure to comply can lead to charges of "fomenting social division," followed by a trial and a prison sentence lasting months or years. If the leader persists after release, they are added to a list and may end up being found dead by the side of the road.

While so far, none of the Iranian disciples I know have been imprisoned or killed, the risk is always there. Every time they share the gospel, gather around the Word, or worship secretly, they face danger. Similarly, in the Texas prisons, every gang member who turns to Christ counts the cost, asking himself, *What will my gang do to me if I leave?*

Jesus taught his disciples not to fear people who can kill the body, but to fear God, who loves them and counts the hairs on their head (Matthew 10:28–31). He prepared us for the reality that family and friends will betray and hate us. We will be brought before the authorities. But we will not be alone; the Holy Spirit will teach us what to say (Luke 12:11–12). Jesus' predictions were fulfilled in Acts and continue to be fulfilled around the world today.

The book of Acts reveals a recurring pattern—miracles and gospel preaching lead to new disciples and churches, followed by persecution. Persecution always results in planting a new church. The messengers suffer, but the Word keeps advancing.

Stephen was the first to die for his faith in Jesus. In his final moments, he looked up and saw the Son of Man standing at God's right hand. Stephen discovered he wasn't alone (Acts 7:55–56). Similarly, Paul and Silas, after being beaten, bruised, and chained with their legs locked in wooden stocks, were found worshipping God at midnight (Acts 16:24–25). They too discovered they weren't alone. Jesus was with them.

We follow a crucified Lord who won his victory through weakness. He suffered, and therefore we suffer. The secret to success in the face of persecution is not natural bravery—in the garden, Jesus' own disciples fled in fear. Instead, the secret lies in discovering we are not alone.

Read Acts 7:54–60; 8:1–3; 11:19.

● What do we learn about God from this story?

● What do we learn about people?

● What do we learn about persecution and movements?

● What do you need to do to obey what you've learned?

5

Deeper

A Movement of Priests

In Rajasthan, India, I met an eighty-year-old grandmother who cannot read or write. Yet she shares her story, proclaims the gospel, prays for the sick, recites Scripture, makes disciples, baptizes them, and teaches them to follow Christ. I also met a young woman who has been doing the same work alongside her father since she was twelve. From an illiterate grandmother to a daughter who began as a girl, whole families embody the priesthood of believers. This is what sets movements apart: *Everyone* joins in the work.

When Jesus called fishermen to be his disciples, he called them to follow him and fish for others (Matthew 4:18–20). He gave them something to do. These men were ordinary and unqualified. The woman at the well became the first missionary to her Samaritan village (John 4). The demoniac was the first missionary to the Decapolis (Luke 8:38–39).

God chose all Israel to be a kingdom of priests, a holy nation that, through their obedience to the covenant, would bear witness to him throughout the world (Exodus 19:4–6). Tragically, Israel fell well short of God's intention. Jesus fulfilled God's plan for Israel and established a renewed Israel, composed of Jews and Gentiles who put their faith in the Messiah (Ephesians 2).

Christ is our Priest, and all believers share in his priesthood through union with him. There is no priestly class. Jesus gave the Great Commission to every disciple. Our Priest and risen Lord gave us the authority to make disciples of the nations by going, baptizing, and teaching them to obey everything he has commanded (Matthew 28:16–20).

The royal priesthood is evident in Acts as the priests of the new covenant baptize, pray, worship, read and obey the Scriptures, love one another, celebrate the Lord's Supper, give sacrificially, and proclaim the gospel from Jerusalem to the world (Acts 2:36–47).

This is what Peter means when he says, "You are a chosen people, a royal priesthood, a holy nation, God's special possession, that you may declare the praises of him who called you out of darkness into his wonderful light" (1 Peter 2:9).

In John's vision of heaven, he sees the Lamb that was slain who, with his blood, has purchased people from every tribe and language and people and nation. For what purpose? That they would be a kingdom and priests to serve our God forever (Revelation 5:9–10).

The gospel goes out in the power of the Spirit through these royal priests as God gathers his people from every tribe and language. For all eternity, they will be a kingdom of priests, God's chosen people, proclaiming his glory.

Read Romans 16:1–16, 21–23.

● What do we learn about God from this story?

____

____

____

● What do we learn about people?

____

____

____

● What do we learn about a movement of priests?

____

____

____

● What do you need to do to obey what you've learned?

____

____

____

6

Deeper

The Person of Peace

In Laos, Peter went looking for a person of peace—a receptive individual who would open the door to their community. Peter found this person in Daw, who then secretly gathered other families to hear what Peter came to share. Daw became the first disciple in his village. As Peter continued to train and disciple him, Daw grew into the village's first evangelist, disciple maker, and church planter. The outcome was an indigenous movement of disciples and churches.

Peter pursued this strategy by following the model Jesus set. Near the end of Jesus' journey to Jerusalem, to fulfill his mission to seek and to save the lost, Jesus deliberately invited himself to stay at Zacchaeus's house (Luke 19:1–10). When Jesus left, Zacchaeus remained as a transformed witness to his community. Jesus modeled what he taught his disciples to do. His encounter with Zacchaeus parallels the instructions he gave to the Seventy-Two before sending them out (Luke 10:1–11; 19:1–10). The purpose of their mission was to find receptive households before moving on to the next village.

Following the day of Pentecost, the movement of God spread from Jerusalem to Rome primarily because Jesus' disciples followed his example and teaching about using receptive households as doorways into communities.

Author David Matson points out that in Acts, "Household conversion stories provide several firsts in bringing salvation to the unreached peoples of the world: the first Gentile man (Cornelius), the first Gentile woman (Lydia), the first pagan (the Roman jailer), the first synagogue ruler (Crispus). Their conversions led to even more Gentiles coming to faith. Each resulted in a new church."[1]

These examples from Acts demonstrate a consistent principle: People are more likely to adopt the faith of those closest to them. As the number of converted friends and family increases, so does the likelihood of conversion. But there is more to it than good sociology. It's consistent with who God is. God is Father, Son and Holy Spirit—eternally in community. Made in his image, we are social beings. That's why the gospel spreads through social networks as God goes before the messengers, preparing the way.

God led Jesus to both Zacchaeus and the woman at the well, preparing their hearts for their encounter with Jesus. Similarly, God prepared both Peter and Cornelius for their meeting, ensuring that Peter arrived to a full house of Cornelius's friends and family—a gathering that made church formation far more likely.

We see this played out in movements today. In Indonesia, workers prioritize households and groups rather than individuals. In Lebanon, Ibrahim repented and believed and followed Jesus. He was a person of peace, having been spiritually prepared and waiting for the messenger God had promised to send. At first, his family was suspicious, but they were won over once they saw his transformed life. One by one, they joined him, and the gospel spread throughout his clan. From this receptive household, the movement grew to other clans and networks across the region. Every multiplying movement I know employs this principle.

Read Acts 16:6–40.

● What do we learn about God from this story?

____

____

____

● What do we learn about people?

____

____

____

● What do we learn about movements and the person of peace?

____

____

____

● What do you need to do to obey what you've learned?

____

____

____

7

Deeper

The Outsider–Insider Partnership

In the book of Acts, Luke doesn't record any mission trips by Paul beyond Ephesus, so it's widely assumed Paul was in the city for up to three years. Yet, through the disciples he trained, "all the Jews and Greeks who lived in the province of Asia heard the word of the Lord" (Acts 19:10). In Ephesus, Paul worked as an outsider who trained and sent out insiders throughout all of Asia Minor. One insider was Epaphras, who planted churches in the Lycus Valley in the cities of Laodicea, Hierapolis, and Colossae.

Many movements have started with a partnership between an external catalyst and an internal leader. When Don Waybright entered Darrington Prison, Texas, he intended to train disciples to follow Christ and make disciples. He aimed to start a movement that he would not lead—a strategy rooted in his complete confidence in the Word and the Spirit, as well as the clarity of the core missionary task. He provided disciples in prisons with a clear 4-Fields strategy and simple yet effective methods.[1] Don watched for disciples who quickly obeyed and built coaching relationships with them. His focus was on those who shared the vision for a movement of disciples and churches. He coached inside leaders like David Ludwick to take ownership of the core missionary task. As they stepped forward, Don stepped back.

This outsider–insider partnership is a recurring pattern in all our case studies. The same pattern can be seen as Jesus prepared his disciples for his departure.

In India, God brought Gary and Ravi together in an outsider–insider relationship. They were drawn together by their uncompromising commitment to the Great Commission and developed a father-and-son bond. For over seven years, they persisted in refining their methods before achieving a breakthrough. Through the struggle, God shaped their identities.

In Ghana, outsiders Terry and Amy Ruff teamed up with insider Isaac, addressing challenges related to strategy and methods. Although breakthroughs led to growth, Terry recognized that movements require more than just the correct strategy and processes. He took on a father-figure role to confront Isaac's moral failure, which was a critical identity issue rooted in disobeying God's Word and resisting the Holy Spirit. Isaac turned back and was restored.

We see the same outsider–insider pattern in Lebanon with James and Ibrahim. Though James is the outsider, he is half Ibrahim's age and treats him like a father. Their relationship works because both men practice humility.

Outsiders are clear about their identity, confident in the Word and the Spirit, and committed to the core missionary task. They are not trying to promote their ministry; they are looking for inside leaders. Insiders are resilient and eager to learn. They take responsibility for the core missionary task and demonstrate this through their actions. They are the ones who say, "If no one else will do this, I will!"—even if they don't know how! Outsiders and insiders are drawn to each other because they share a common heart. Once the partnership is established, they spend significant time together.

For a generation, most movements were built through an outsider–insider partnership, with the outsider often a Westerner. However, outsiders from the non-Western world are now replacing them. Movement practitioner and strategist Stan Parks observes that movements are now "cascading from their initial peoples and places into other peoples and places, both near and far."[2]

Globally, over 90 percent of new movements in the last five to ten years were started by teams sent out from existing movements—without any involvement from Western cross-cultural workers.[3] It's not the end of the outsider–insider roles; rather, it signifies the end of reliance on the West.

This is what we hope to see: movements initiating other movements, no longer relying solely on dependence but working together in partnership to fulfill the Great Commission.

Read Acts 20:4, 17–38.

● What do we learn about God from this story?

____

____

____

● What do we learn about people?

____

____

____

● What do we learn about developing inside leaders in movements?

____

____

____

● What do you need to do to obey what you've learned?

____

____

____

8

Deeper

Church and the Movement of God

Our mission begins with making disciples but is not complete until those disciples are formed into a community.

When Troy and Rick first met Shane and his two friends in California, they didn't just teach them; they walked alongside them in discipleship. Then they equipped them to reach their relationships and challenged them to form the new disciples into a church.

God wants a people who will display his glory to the world, now and into eternity.

From the beginning, God's purpose in calling Abraham was that he would father a nation that would become a witness to the nations (Genesis 12:1–3). That vision was fulfilled in the coming of Jesus, who embodied faithful Israel.

The call to follow Jesus was a call to form communities of his disciples. Jesus taught his disciples what it means to follow him together. He taught them to obey his commands. He taught them to live a life of love, forgiveness, generosity, and servanthood. He taught them to proclaim the good news of God's reign and to make disciples. He taught them to pray and expect God to answer. He taught them not to fear persecution. He taught them to baptize new disciples and to celebrate the Lord's Supper together. Most of all, he taught them who he is—Messiah, Lord, and Savior of the world. The identity of the people of God was formed from the life and mission of Jesus.

Luke provides us with a clear picture of the life of the first church as God's intention for all churches (Acts 2:36–47). He shows us how churches should function. They are devoted to the apostles' teaching, to each other, and to prayer. They gather publicly and from house to house, sharing meals, experiencing the power of the Spirit. They meet the needs of the poor within the community.

In Texas, prisoners gather daily in day rooms to pray and worship, share their burdens and breakthroughs, study the Scriptures, celebrate the Lord's Supper, and give to those in need. They are not just a Bible study; they are the body of Christ, the people of God, the new Israel.

In a movement, the task doesn't end with a profession of faith but continues to the obedience of faith in a community of disciples. There's no evangelism without discipleship and no discipleship without church formation.

In Acts, wherever the gospel finds faith, churches are formed from Jerusalem to the ends of the earth. The core missionary task is about taking the gospel to every people and every place, forming new disciples into churches to the glory of God.

Read Acts 2:36–47.

● What do we learn about God from this story?

____

____

____

● What do we learn about people?

____

____

____

● What do we learn about church and the movement of God?

____

____

____

● What do you need to do to obey what you've learned?

____

____

____

Deeper

Money and Movements

Trading his work as a carpenter for the roads of Galilee, Jesus called his first disciples to leave their nets and follow him as he taught them how to fish for others. Together, they traveled light, supported by the hospitality of receptive people (Luke 10:5–7), the financial gifts of a group of wealthy women (Luke 8:3), and, at times, through miraculous provision (Luke 9:10–17).

When his disciples were sent out, Jesus told them to leave their wallets behind, trusting God to provide through the people who welcomed them and their message (Luke 10:1–11). Jesus did not leave detailed instructions for funding the movement. Instead, he set an example and gave his disciples his Word, the Holy Spirit, and the missionary task, promising that as they went to the ends of the earth, he would always be with them (Matthew 28:18–20).[1]

Paul didn't want to be a burden on new disciples, so he worked with his hands to support himself and his coworkers (Acts 20:34). However, he accepted gifts from believers and established churches if the money came without strings attached (Philippians 4:10–20). There were times he was unable to work to support himself, especially when he was in custody or in a location for a short time.

In a movement, no one is paid to do what every disciple should naturally do. Ordinary disciples share the gospel, make disciples, and plant churches without pay. You can't pay enough people to create a disciple making movement. Volunteers do most of the work in any movement, not professionals.

Consider the example in Rajasthan, India, where an extended household of grandparents, three brothers, and their families helped one brother travel to an unreached area for three months. During the day, he worked in the fields. At night, he planted churches. They didn't seek or need any outside support or permission. The movement was internally funded by sacrifice and shared vision.

Movements fund multiplication, not addition. Addition means paying someone to plant a single church. Multiplication involves funding leaders who multiply disciples, leaders, and churches. Funding includes a living allowance and expenses, such as transportation or the cost of moving to a new, unreached region. Salaries are reserved for movement catalysts responsible for multiple streams of churches. Some movements have thousands of churches and yet have fewer than thirty catalysts receiving salaries.

In the New Testament, Peter's clash with Simon the sorcerer is a powerful illustration of Jesus' teaching that you cannot serve both God and money (Acts 8:9–24). Leaders who exploit their position for personal gain and power will corrupt a movement. The oxygen of a movement is the commitment of its people—to give, to go, to serve without pay, to open their homes, to work with their hands, and to trust that God goes with them.

Read Luke 10:1–11.

● What do we learn about God from this story?

● What do we learn about people?

● What do we learn about money and movements?

● What do you need to do to obey what you've learned?

10

Deeper

Creator and Lord

In 1979, when God handed Iran over to an Islamic revolution, there were about five hundred Muslim-background believers. A generation later, following widespread disillusionment with radical Islam, there are now over 1 million Muslim-background disciples of Jesus.

What began as the Arab Spring became the Arab Winter as wars spread across the Middle East. Yet amid the turmoil, unprecedented movements of disciples and churches are multiplying across the Muslim world. I met some movement catalysts who were experiencing rapid growth in the Muslim world. When I asked them what they were learning, they told me they were learning to "move toward the chaos." God is at work in the chaos of human history.

This pattern of God working through human turmoil is consistent with Scripture. From Genesis to Revelation, the pages of the Bible reveal the one true God: Creator and Lord of history.[1] God chose Israel to be a light to the nations (Isaiah 49:6). He promised blessing for faithfulness to the covenant and judgment for disobedience (Deuteronomy 28). Either way, Israel was to be a witness to the world.

The way God dealt with Israel sheds light on how he deals with all nations. He determines their rise and fall according to his purposes (Exodus 9:16). Israel's example and God's response send a message to the nations that they too will be held accountable. Judgment in history was never meant to be final, but the road back to a relationship with God.

170

Although we cannot always discern his ways, God is constantly at work in the lives of nations and individuals, judging evil and promoting what is right.

Jesus warned Jerusalem that rejecting him would bring God's judgment, culminating in the destruction of the Temple and the city. That judgment fell in AD 70 as a warning, intended not only for Israel, but for the whole world. Individuals and peoples are responsible to God for their response to Jesus and his messengers (Matthew 25:31–46).

Paul reminds us that God's judgment is a present reality: "The wrath of God is being revealed from heaven against all the godlessness and wickedness of people, who suppress the truth by their wickedness" (Romans 1:18). God's judgments in this life anticipate and warn of the final judgment. He intervenes repeatedly throughout history. This redeeming judgment falls on nations and on individuals. For instance, after Herod Agrippa murdered James and persecuted Peter, an angel struck him down when he refused to rebuke the crowd for hailing him as a god (Acts 12:1–4, 22–23).

Our faith must be defined by God's sovereignty over nations and history. Given the scarcity of multiplying movements in the Western world, and knowing that he is Lord of the harvest, our response should take three forms. First, we continue to do what is right, following Jesus' example in entering unreached fields, proclaiming the gospel, making disciples, forming healthy churches, and multiplying leaders. We follow his example. Second, we discern God's present work and learn from those exceptions, such as what God is doing in Texas prisons or in Southern California. Third, through it all, we remember that God holds the nations in the palm of his hand. The same God who shook the Muslim world will shake the Western world. We need to be ready.

Read Acts 4:23–31.

● What do we learn about God from this story?

____

____

____

● What do we learn about people?

____

____

____

● What do we learn about God's sovereignty and movements?

____

____

____

● What do you need to do to obey what you've learned?

____

____

____

Acknowledgments

This is my fourth title with Anna Robinson as editor. Working with her has been a joy.
I'd also like to thank my good friends at e3 Partners for believing in this project and covering the cost of my travel.

Appendix 1

Strategy

The 4-Fields

Strategy

The 4-Fields answers five questions:

1. Entry: How do I enter a new field?
2. Gospel: What do I say?
3. Discipleship: How do I make disciples?
4. Church: How will I form healthy churches?
5. Leaders: How do I multiply leaders?

movements.net/4fields

4-Fields Discovery

Passage:

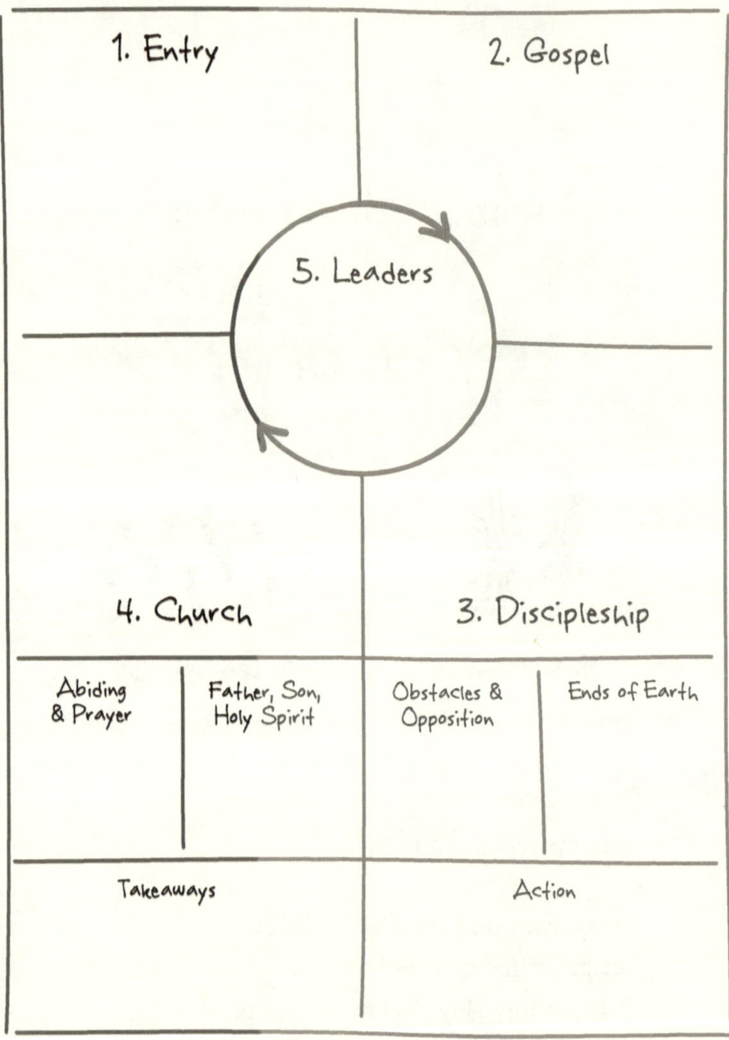

4-Fields Discovery

Fill out the 4-Fields Worksheet for each chapter of Acts or one of the Gospels.

1. Entry: Where and how do they engage people?

2. Gospel: What is their message?

3. Discipleship: How do they make disciples?

4. Church: How do they start and strengthen communities of disciples?

5. Leaders: How do they reproduce leaders?

- **Abiding and Prayer:** How do they go deeper with God through prayer and surrender?

- **Father, Son, and Holy Spirit:** What is the evidence of God's activity?

- **Obstacles and Opposition:** What hardships and opposition do they face?

- **Ends of the Earth:** How does the Word spread to every place and every people?

- **Takeaways;** What has God shown you?

- **Action:** What will you do?

Appendix 2

Methods

The 411

This training answers *four* questions, on *one* sheet of paper, in *one* hour (411):

1. Why do we make disciples?
2. Who do we reach?
3. What do we say?
4. When will we do it?

movements.net/411

The Commands of Christ

The Commands of Christ are Discovery Bible Studies for initial discipleship. They use the 3-Thirds process below as the pattern of learning:

1. Repent and Believe: A Sinful Woman (Luke 7:36–50)
2. Be Baptized: The Ethiopian Eunuch (Acts 8:26–39)
3. Pray: The Lord's Prayer (Matthew 6:9–13)
4. Make Disciples: The Samaritan Woman (John 4:4–42)
5. Love: The Good Samaritan (Luke 10:25–37)
6. Worship: Paul and Silas (Acts 16:25–34)
7. Celebrate: Lord's Supper (Luke 22:7–20; 1 Corinthians 11:23–29)

8. Give: The Generous Widow (Mark 12:41–44)

9. Gather: The First Church (Acts 2:36–47)

Ongoing discipleship involves either book-by-book or thematic studies of the Scriptures using the 3-Thirds process.

nplsimpletools.com

3-Thirds Discipleship

This is the building block for discipleship. The pattern is applied to disciple pre-believers, new disciples, maturing disciples, and leaders.

First Third	Second Third	Final Third

1. Mutual care
 	
2. Worship
	5. New lesson
	• Discovery Bible Study
	  – Read the text and retell it in your own words.
	  – What does the passage teach us about God?
	  – What does it teach us about people?
	  – Is there a command to obey or an example to follow? And/or a new skill?
		7. Set goals
		• How will you obey what you've learned?
		• Who could you share with?

3. Loving accountability • Have you done what you committed to do last time? **4. Vision**	**6. Practice the new learning**	**8. Commissioning and prayer**

youtu.be/cEiLWwJb-lo

Church Circle

Disciples identify the characteristics of a healthy church (Acts 2:36–47). They place a symbol within the circle if they are fulfilling that function. The symbol is outside the circle if they are not displaying that function. A dotted circle represents a discipleship group that has not yet committed to being a church together. A solid line shows the group has committed to being a church.

> Those who repent and believe are added to the church.

Disciples are baptized and have the authority to baptize.

Prayer: Corporate and individual prayer.

Disciples are trained to share the gospel.

Love for one another expressed in deeds.

Worship: Corporate and individual worship.

Regular celebration of the Lord's Supper.

Giving to those in need and for the spread of the gospel.

Learning obedience to God's Word.

Recognized local leaders.

A dotted line circle indicates a group. A solid circle indicates the group identifies as a church.

obeychrist.com/tools/church-circle

MAWL

- *Model*: Show them how to do it.
- *Assist:* Help them do it.
- *Watch*: Provide feedback.
- *Leave*: Entrust them with the work.

youtu.be/Fcxmu1gtyVs

Appendix 3

The 5-Levels of Leadership

The 5-Levels of Leadership

L1	L2	L3	L4	L5
Seed Sower	Church Planter	Church Multiplier	Multiplication Trainer	Movement Catalyst

← Addition | Multiplication →

A disciple who	A level 1 leader who	A level 2 leader who	A level 3 leader who	A level 4 leader who
• spreads the gospel among family and friends • masters simple, effective tools for sharing the gospel • loves lost people • models seed sowing to others	• learns how to make disciples and plant churches • trains level 1 workers to share the gospel • forms disciples into groups that become churches	• starts churches that reproduce churches to four generations • equips level 1 and level 2 leaders • ensures the health of churches and releases authority to local leaders	• produces four generations of new churches across multiple streams of church planting • engages beyond the leader's own network to cast vision and train for multiplication • identifies and resolves barriers to multiplication	• becomes a catalyst for multiple streams of church planting among unreached people groups • equips level 3 and level 4 leaders to facilitate multiple streams of multiple generations of church planting • majors in networking, resourcing and vision casting

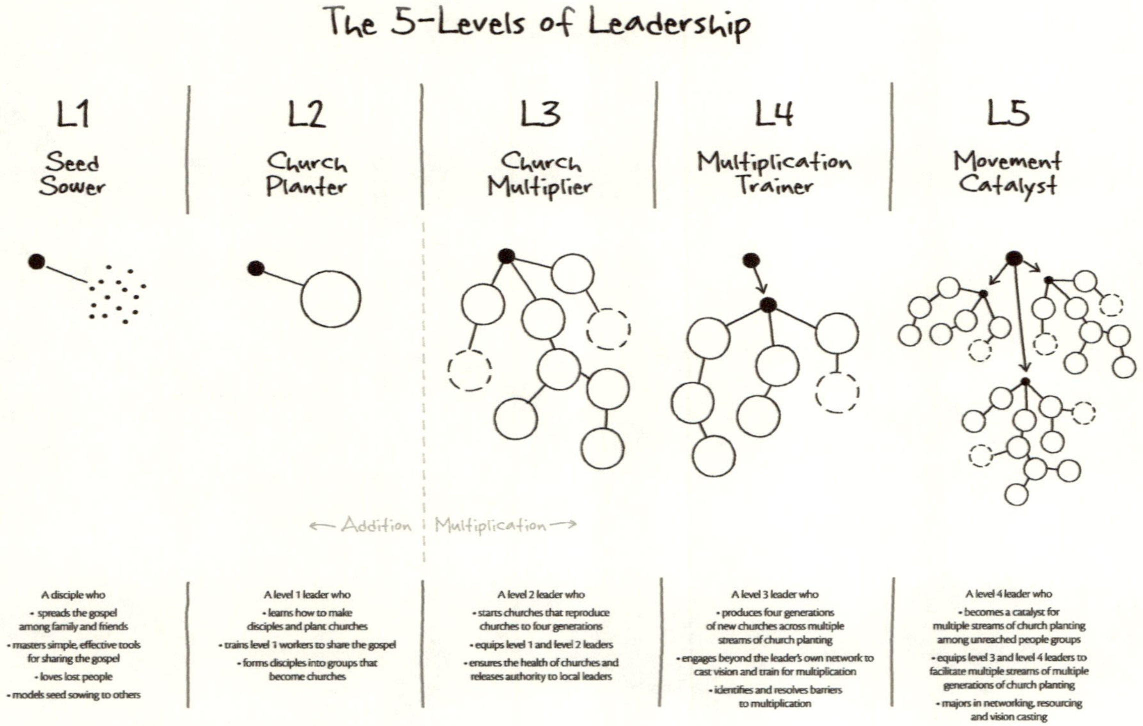

youtu.be/RebN24RWMRQ

Steve Addison, *Pioneering Movements: Leadership That Multiplies Disciples and Churches* (IVP, 2015).

Bibliography

Addison, Steve. "320-James and Hope: The Call." *Movements*. Podcast. January 29, 2024. https://www.movements.net/blog/blog/2024/1/29/320-james-and-hope-the-call-mjbzb.

Addison, Steve. "321-James and Hope: The Work." *Movements*. Podcast. February 8, 2024. https://www.movements.net/blog/blog/2024/1/29/321-james-and-hope-the-work-9n2st.

Addison, Steve. "331-On the Road in South Asia." *Movements*. Podcast. July 5, 2024. https://www.movements.net/blog/331-on-the-road-in-south-asia.

Addison, Steve. "332-Trevor's Story." *Movements*. Podcast. August 14, 2024. https://www.movements.net/blog/332-trevors-story.

Addison, Steve. "344-Diar and Miriam's Story." *Movements*. Podcast. February 6, 2025. https://www.movements.net/blog/344-diar-and-miriams-story.

Addison, Steve. "345-Coaching from the Sidelines." *Movements*. Podcast. March 2, 2025. https://www.movements.net/blog/345-coaching-from-the-sidelines.

Addison, Steve. "346-When Instant Success Takes Decades." *Movements*. Podcast. March 12, 2025. https://www.movements.net/blog/345-sometimes-instant-success-takes-decades.

Addison, Steve. "357-Joe and Dawn's Story." *Movements*. Podcast. September 4, 2025. https://www.movements.net/blog/357-joe-and-dawns-story.

Addison, Steve. *Acts and the Movement of God: From Jerusalem to the Ends of the Earth*. 100Movements Publishing, 2023.

Addison, Steve. "The Continuing Ministry of the Apostle in the Church's Mission." Fuller Theological Seminary, 1995.

Addison, Steve. "Don Waybright Baptises Jesus in Prison." *Movements*. Accessed August 25, 2025. https://www.movements.net/blog/blog/2017/6/28/don-waybright-baptises-jesus-in-prison-ymdwm.

Addison, Steve. "Gospel Changes Life of 108-Year-Old." Accessed September 2, 2025. https://www.imb.org/2022/06/23/gospel-changes-life-of-108-year-old/.

Addison, Steve. *Movements That Change the World: Five Keys to Spreading the Gospel*. Revised. IVP, 2011.

Addison, Steve. *Pioneering Movements: Leadership That Multiplies Disciples and Churches*. IVP, 2015.

Addison, Steve. *The Rise and Fall of Movements: A Roadmap for Leaders*. 100Movements Publishing, 2019.

Addison, Steve. *What Jesus Started: Joining the Movement, Changing the World*. IVP, 2012.

Addison, Steve. *Your Part in God's Story: 40 Days from Genesis to Revelation*. 100Movements Publishing, 2021.

Addison, Steve, and David Bareham. "178-Becoming a Great Commission Church." *Movements*. Podcast. November 29, 2018. https://www.movements.net/blog/blog/2018/11/15/178-a-local-church-takes-on-the-great-commission-ntw55?rq=178.

Addison, Steve, and Troy Cooper. "285-LA Update." *Movements*. Podcast. October 24, 2022. https://www.movements.net/blog/blog/2022/10/19/285-la-update-8hzt5.

Addison, Steve, Troy Cooper, Max and Sydnie Doty, and Jordan Giusti. "280-Mobbing for Movements." *Movements*. Podcast. August 5, 2022. https://www.movements.net/blog/blog/2022/8/5/280-mobbing-for-movements-yjd43.

Addison, Steve, Troy Cooper, and Jordan Giusti. "259-California Update." *Movements*. Podcast. October 14, 2021. https://www.movements.net/blog/blog/2021/10/14/259-california-update-mg776.

Addison, Steve, and Max and Sydnie Doty. "340-Max and Sydnie's Story." *Movements*. Podcast. November 27, 2024. https://www.movements.net/blog/340-max-and-sydnies-story.

Addison, Steve, and Nick and Sarah Field. "353-NoPlaceLeft New Zealand." *Movements*. Podcast. July 16, 2025. https://www.movements.net/blog/353-noplaceleft-new-zealand.

Addison, Steve, and Troop Foster. "349-Troop's Story." *Movements*. Podcast. May 8, 2025. https://www.movements.net/blog/349-troops-story.

Addison, Steve, and Bruce Hackett. "365-NoPlaceLeft on Campus." *Movements*. Podcast. January 22, 2026. https://www.movements.net/blog/365-noplaceleft-on-campus.

Addison, Steve, and Shane and Graciela Narissian. "341-Zeal Church." *Movements*. Podcast. December 12, 2024. https://www.movements.net/blog/341-zeal-church.

Addison, Steve, and Terry and Amy Ruff. "194-Multiplying Movements in West Africa." *Movements*. Podcast. June 27, 2019. https://www.

movements.net/blog/blog/2019/6/18/194-multiplying-movements-in-west-africa-sa3ez.

Addison, Steve, and Terry Solley. "324-Release to the Captives." *Movements*. Podcast. March 25, 2024. https://www.movements.net/blog/324-release-to-the-captives.

Addison, Steve, and Glenn and Rhonda Stewart. "292-A Movement of God in Rajasthan (1)." *Movements*. Podcast. February 3, 2023. https://www.movements.net/blog/blog/2023/2/2/292-a-movement-of-god-in-rajasthan-1-49tm4.

Addison, Steve, and Glenn and Rhonda Stewart. "293-A Movement of God in Rajasthan (2)." *Movements*. Podcast. February 10, 2023. https://www.movements.net/blog/blog/2023/2/10/293-a-movement-of-god-in-rajasthan-2-wr3se.

Addison, Steve, JT Timblin, and Troy Cooper. "237-LA Breakthroughs." *Movements*. Podcast. December 9, 2020. https://www.movements.net/blog/blog/2020/12/9/237-la-breakthroughs-zga9l.

Addison, Steve, and Don Waybright. "342-A Glimpse of Heaven on Death Row." *Movements*. Podcast. January 7, 2025. https://www.movements.net/blog/342a-glimpse-of-heaven-on-death-row.

"Christianity in Iran." Wikipedia. Last Modified November 25, 2022. https://en.wikipedia.org/w/index.php?title=Christianity_in_Iran&oldid=1123705386.

Clinton, J. Robert. *The Making of a Leader: Recognizing the Lessons and Stages of Leadership Development*. Revised. NavPress, 2014.

Cole, Carolyn. "Beach Baptisms Draw Large Gatherings to the Shore." *Los Angeles Times*, August 13, 2020.

Cooper, Troy. "4Fields Discovery: Gospels and Acts." *Movements*. Accessed March 12, 2018. https://www.movements.net/5-leaders.

Cooper, Troy. "Church Circles Discovery: Epistles." *Movements*. Accessed March 12, 2018. https://www.movements.net/5-leaders.

Cooper, Troy, dir. *The Brutal Facts*. n.d. Accessed September 3, 2025. https://www.youtube.com/watch?v=rw4tk6xBZE4.

Corley, Felix. "Obituary: Haik Hovsepian Mehr." *The Independent*, February 1, 1994. https://www.independent.co.uk/news/people/obituary-haik-hovsepian-mehr-1391238.html.

Cunningham, Scott. *"Through Many Tribulations" The Theology of Persecution in Luke-Acts*. Journal for the Study of the New Testament Supplement Series 142. Sheffield Academic Press, 1997.

Dale, Patrick. "Lecture Surveying Redeeming Judgment: The Judgments of God in the Biblical Story and the Evolution of the Understanding of Judgment." Accessed September 22, 2025. https://www.gtu.edu/sites/default/files/docs/news/Dale-Patrick-Lecture-Redeeming-Judgment.pdf.

DeYoung, Kevin, and Greg Gilbert. *What Is the Mission of the Church?: Making Sense of Social Justice, Shalom, and the Great Commission.* Crossway Books, 2011.

Dubois, William J., Stan Parks, and Justin Long. *Forests in the Seed: How Kingdom Movements Are Multiplying Across the Unreached World.* Patmos Education Group, 2024.

Ek Rasta. "Ek Rasta South Asia." Accessed September 2, 2025. https://southasiansands.wixsite.com/ekrasta.

Ferdinando, Keith. "Mission: A Problem of Definition." *Themelios* 33:1 (2008): 46–59.

Fesko, J. V. "The Priesthood of All Believers." The Gospel Coalition. Accessed September 16, 2025. https://www.thegospelcoalition.org/essay/the-priesthood-of-all-believers/.

Garrison, David. *Inside Church Planting Movements: What 25 Years of Assessments Reveal.* WIGTake Resources, 2025.

Garrison, David. *A Wind in the House of Islam: How God Is Drawing Muslims Around the World to Faith in Jesus Christ.* WIGTake Resources, 2014.

Hartley, Karen. "Biography of Haik Hovsepian-Mehr." *Truett Journal of Church and Mission* 2/1 (Spring 2004): 43–57.

Howell, Don N. Jr. "Confidence in the Spirit as the Governing Ethos of the Pauline Mission." In *The Holy Spirit and Mission Dynamics*, edited by C. Douglas McConnell. Evangelical Missiological Series 5. William Carey Library, 1997.

"Incarceration in the United States." Wikipedia. Last modified August 22, 2025. https://en.wikipedia.org/w/index.php?title=Incarceration_in_the_United_States&oldid=1307258070.

"Jakarta." Wikipedia. Last modified August 23, 2025. https://en.wikipedia.org/w/index.php?title=Jakarta&oldid=1307368651.

Larson, Trevor. *Focus on the Fruit! Movement Case Studies & Fruitful Practices.* Published independently, 2018.

Lewis, C. S. *The Problem of Pain.* HarperCollins, 1940.

Long, Justin. "How Long to Reach the Goal?" *Beyond.* January 25, 2023. https://beyond.org/2023/01/25/how-long-to-reach-the-goal/.

"Malay Language." Wikipedia. Last modified August 22, 2025. https://en.wikipedia.org/w/index.php?title=Malay_language&oldid=1307225167.

Mandryk, Jason. *Operation World: The Definitive Prayer Guide to Every Nation*. 7th ed. Biblica, 2010.

Markarian, Krikor. "Today's Iranian Revolution: How the Mullahs Are Leading the Nation to Jesus." *Mission Frontiers* September–October (2008): 6–13.

Matson, David. *Household Conversion Narratives in Acts: Pattern and Interpretation*. Sheffield Academic Press, 1996.

Miller, Duane Alexander. "Power, Personalities and Politics: The Growth of Iranian Christianity since 1979." *Mission Studies* 32 (2015). https://doi.org/10.1163/15733831-12341380.

Monnig, Matthew S. "Satan in Lukan Narrative and Theology: Human Agency in the Conflict between the Authority of Satan and the Power of God." PhD diss. Duke University, 2019.

NoPlaceLeft International Coalition. "7 Phases." December 29, 2021. https://noplaceleft.net/7-phases/.

NPL Simple Tools. "NPL Simple Tools: 4-Fields." Accessed August 22, 2025. https://www.nplsimpletools.com/4-fields.

Parks, Stan. "Cascading Gospel: Movements Starting Movements." *Mission Frontiers*, February 2023, 8–11.

Patrick, Dale. *Redeeming Judgment*. n.d.

"Religion in Laos." Wikipedia. Last modified July 30, 2025. https://en.wikipedia.org/w/index.php?title=Religion_in_Laos&oldid=1303357947.

Schnabel, Eckhard J. *Acts*. Edited by Clinton Arnold. Zondervan Exegetical Commentary on the New Testament. Zondervan, 2012.

Schreiner, Patrick. *The Mission of the Triune God: A Theology of Acts*. Crossway, 2022.

Schrock, David S. *The Royal Priesthood and the Glory of God*. Short Studies in Biblical Theology. Crossway, 2022.

Shank, Nathan. "Generational Mapping: Tracking Elements of Church Formation Within CPM's." *Mission Frontiers*, December 2012, 26–30.

Shank, Nathan, and Kari. *The Four Fields: A Manual for Church Planting Facilitation*. 2015. https://www.movements.net/4fields.

Shipman, Mike. *Any-3: Anyone, Anywhere, Any Time: Lead Muslims To Christ Now!* WIGTake Resources, 2013.

Spencer, F. Scott. *Journeying through Acts: A Literary-Cultural Reading*. Baker Academic, 2004.

Statista. "Number of Prisoners in the U.S., by State 2022." Accessed August 8, 2025. https://www.statista.com/statistics/203757/number-of-prisoners-in-the-us-by-states/.

"The Commands of Christ." Accessed August 22, 2025. https://www.obeychrist.com/.

"UPG Engaged through Ek Rasta SD Cards." Accessed August 22, 2025. https://www.imb.org/2022/06/23/upg-engaged-through-ek-rasta-sd-cards/.

Watson, David. "Discovering God: Field Testing Guide v2.0." 2008.

Watson, David L., and Paul D. Watson. *Contagious Disciple Making: Leading Others on a Journey of Discovery*. Thomas Nelson, 2014.

Notes

Foreword

[1] Christianity growing faster than the general population might be attributed to one of two causes: biological growth or disciples multiplying at a rate beyond general population growth. While migration is at times a significant cause for growth among a Christian community, migration of Christians to a new host area assumes migration away from another.

Introduction: A Time to Risk

[1] William J. Dubois, Stan Parks, and Justin Long, *Forests in the Seed: How Kingdom Movements Are Multiplying Across the Unreached World* (Patmos Education Group, 2024), 17.

[2] Dubois, Parks, and Long, *Forests in the Seed*, 17. See also David Garrison, *Inside Church Planting Movements: What 25 Years of Assessments Reveal* (WIGTake Resources, 2025).

[3] I've dealt with these at length in Steve Addison, *The Rise and Fall of Movements: A Roadmap for Leaders* (100Movements Publishing, 2019).

[4] This outline is known as the 4-Fields—see   one. See also Nathan Shank and Kari Shank, "Four Fields of Kingdom Growth: Starting and Releasing Healthy Churches," *Movements*, 2007; rev. 2014, accessed September 5, 2025, www.movements.net/4fields. See also Steve Addison, *What Jesus Started: Joining the Movement, Changing the World* (InterVarsity Press, 2012).

[5] See the Church Circle in appendix two. 1 A Glimpse of Heaven on Death Row: Texas.

1 A Glimpse of Heaven on Death Row: Texas

[1] For an account of the visit, see Steve Addison and Don Waybright, "342-A Glimpse of Heaven on Death Row," *Movements*, podcast, January 7, 2025, https://www.movements.net/blog/342a-glimpse-of-heaven-on-death-row.

[2] See appendix two.

[3] See appendix three.

4   For more on the 4-Fields, see appendix one. See also "4-Fields," https://www.
    movements.net/4fields (accessed September 3, 2025).

5   Steve Addison and Terry Solley, "324-Release to the Captives," *Movements*,
    March 25, 2024, https://www.movements.net/blog/324-release-to-the-captives.

6   Steve Addison and Troop Foster, "349-Troop's Story," *Movements*, podcast, May
    8, 2025, https://www.movements.net/blog/349-troops-story.

2 Victory Through Tears: Laos

1   See appendix one.

2   See the Church Circle in appendix two.

3   Adapted from "Phases of Progress Within a People Group," NPL, accessed
    November 17, 2025, https://noplaceleft.net/7-phases/.

3 Out of the Classroom, Into the Field: Indonesia

1   See appendix two for more on the 3-Thirds. See also Greater Works Guide,
    accessed November 18, 2025, https://bit.ly/geaterworksguide.

2   Mike Shipman, *Any-3: Anyone, Anywhere, Any Time: Lead Muslims to Christ
    Now!* (WIGTake Resources, 2013).

3   "Malay Language," Wikipedia, last modified November 4, 2025, https://en.wikipedia.
    org/w/index.php?title=Malay_language&oldid=1307225167.

4   See Addison, *The Rise and Fall of Movements*, 59–72.

4 Depth *and* Breadth: India

1   For more on the Jesus film, see Jesus Film Project, accessed December 12, 2025,
    https://www.jesusfilm.org.

2   Not to be confused with the concept of "insider movements" within Islam.

3   This figure varied according to the age of the church. For instance, while only 60
    percent of the newest churches (under two years old) were baptizing, that figure
    rose to 86 percent for churches three to five years old.

5 From the Skatepark to the World: California

1   Steve Addison, JT Timblin, and Troy Cooper, "237-LA Breakthroughs," *Movements*,
    podcast, December 9, 2020, https://www.movements.net/blog/blog/2020/12/9/
    237-la-breakthroughs-zga9l.

2   See appendix one.

3   These resources are outlined in appendix two.

4   For more on the 3-Thirds, see appendix two.

5   See appendix two.

6   For more on the 3-Circles, see appendix two.

7   For more on the movement in Pheonix, Arizona, see Steve Addison, Max Doty, and Sydnie Doty, "361-Update from Max and Sydnie," *Movements*, podcast, November 12, 2025, https://www.movements.net/blog/361-update-from-max-and-sydnie.

8   See appendix one.

9   See also Acts 20:17–38; 1 Timothy 3:1–13; Titus 1:5–9.

6 Follow the Fruit: Indonesia

1   For example, John 9:6; Acts 19:11–12.

2   When they had multiplied to 110 groups, they were trained in disciple making movements by David Watson. They were struck by how similar the model was to what they had already learned by trial and error.

3   Trevor Larson, *Focus on the Fruit: Movement Case Studies & Fruitful Practices* (Published independently, 2018), 15.

4   According to Trevor, "Some understood from the Quran that *Isa Al-Masih* was a miracle worker who healed the sick and raised the dead, was called 'the Word of God' and 'holy,' and 'most exalted in the Last Days.' Islamic traditions taught that Jesus would be Judge in the Last Days. These are good foundational truths to build upon."

5   Acts 9:31; 20:17; Romans 16:5.

6   See appendix two.

7 High Stakes, Deep Faith: Ghana

1   Perspectives USA, accessed January 14, 2026, https://perspectives.org.

2   See appendix two.

3   See "Three Circles Gospel Training," NPL, accessed November 27, 2025, https://noplaceleft.net/3-circles-gospel/; and Shipman, *Any-3*.

4   For more on the Creation-to-Christ story, visit "C2C Story," eDOT, accessed December 1, 2025, https://c2cstory.com.

8 We Are the *Talamiz Al-Masih*: Lebanon

1   See Steve Addison, "321-James and Hope: The Work," *Movements*, podcast, February 8, 2024, https://www.movements.net/blog/blog/2024/1/29/321-james-and-hope-the-work-9n2st. See also Steve Addison, "320-James and Hope: The

Call," *Movements*, podcast, January 29, 2024, https://www.movements.net/blog/blog/2024/1/29/320-james-and-hope-the-call-mjbzb.

[2] See appendix one.

[3] See appendix two.

[4] See appendix two and #NoPlaceLeft, "MAWL—Model Assist Watch Launch," YouTube, April 2, 2016, https://www.youtube.com/watch?v=Fcxmu1gtyVs.

9 Sovereign Lord: Iran

[1] Jason Mandryk, *Operation World: The Definitive Prayer Guide to Every Nation* 7th ed. (Biblica, 2010), 465.

[2] Sources for the story of Haik Hovsepian: Felix Corley, "Obituary: Haik Hovsepian Mehr," *The Independent*, February 1, 1994, https:/www.independent.co.uk/news/people/obituary-haik-hovsepian-mehr-1391238.html; Karen Hartley, "Biography of Haik Hovsepian-Mehr," *Truett Journal of Church and Mission* 2, no. 1 (2004), 43–57. Around 170,000, mostly ethnic Armenians and Assyrians, professed faith in Christ in historic churches. See Duane Alexander Miller, "Power, Personalities and Politics: The Growth of Iranian Christianity since 1979," *Mission Studies* 32 (2015), 66–86.

[3] Miller, "Power, Personalities and Politics," 73.

[4] Mehdi Dibaj was murdered four months later.

[5] Miller, "Power, Personalities and Politics," 74.

[6] The estimates of Christians in Iran vary from 380,000 to 1.5 million. "Christianity in Iran," Wikipedia, last modified November 25, 2022, https://en.wikipedia.org/w/index.php?title=Christianity_in_Iran&oldid=1123705386.

[7] See the Church Circle in appendix two.

[8] Miller, "Power, Personalities and Politics," 81–82.

[9] Miller, "Power, Personalities and Politics," 82–83.

[10] Miller, "Power, Personalities and Politics," 83.

[11] Miller, "Power, Personalities and Politics," 83.

Conclusion: Worth the Risk

[1] For more information on MAWL, see appendix two.

[2] For more information on all these methods, see appendix two.

[3] Three years ago, Max trained Bruce Hackett. Bruce and the workers he trained have planted thirty churches in Phoenix, Arizona. See Steve Addison and Bruce Hackett, "365-NoPlaceLeft on Campus," *Movements*, podcast, January 22, 2026, https://www.movements.net/blog/365-noplaceleft-on-campus.

[4] The Fields tell their story in this interview: Steve Addison, Nick and Sarah Field,

"353-NoPlaceLeft New Zealand," *Movements*, podcast, July 16, 2025, https://www.movements.net/blog/353-noplaceleft-new-zealand.

Deeper: What Do Movements Do?

[1]   See Addison, *The Rise and Fall of Movements*, 125–138.

[2]   Patrick Schreiner, *The Mission of the Triune God: A Theology of Acts* (Crossway, 2022), 24.

[3]   F. Scott Spencer, *Journeying through Acts: A Literary-Cultural Reading* (Baker Academic, 2004), 24.

Deeper: The Battle

[1]   See Luke 4:1–13; 11:18–26; 13:16; 22:3, 31; Acts 10:38; 26:17–18.

Deeper: The Person of Peace

[1]   David Matson, *Household Conversion Narratives in Acts: Pattern and Interpretation* (Sheffield Academic Press, 1996), 187.

Deeper: The Outsider–Insider Partnership

[1]   For more on the 4-Fields strategy, see appendix one.

[2]   Stan Parks, "Cascading Gospel: Movements Starting Movements," *Mission Frontiers*, February 2023, 8. "A survey of movement leaders showed that existing movements have started approximately 90% of newer movements." Dubois et al., *Forests in the Seed*, 204.

[3]   Parks, "Cascading Gospel," 8.

Deeper: Money and Movements

[1]   See also Luke 24:45–49 and Acts 1:8.

Deeper: Creator and Lord

[1]   See Steve Addison, *Your Part in God's Story: 40 Days from Genesis to Revelation* (100Movements Publishing, 2021).

www.ingramcontent.com/pod-product-compliance
Lightning Source LLC
Chambersburg PA
CBHW030914060726
47591CB00005B/1546

9 781955 142779